CISCO

Course Booklet

CCNA Discovery

Working at a Small-to-Medium Business or ISP

Version 4.1

Cisco | Networking Academy
Mind Wide Open

ciscopress.com

CCNA Discovery Course Booklet Working at a Small-to-Medium Business or ISP, Version 4.1

Cisco Networking Academy

Copyright© 2010 Cisco Systems, Inc.

Published by:
Cisco Press
800 East 96th Street
Indianapolis, IN 46240 USA

Printed in the United States of America

First Printing   October 2009

Library of Congress Cataloging-in-Publication Data is on file.

ISBN-13: 978-1-58713-253-7

ISBN-10: 1-58713-253-2

Warning and Disclaimer

This book is designed to provide information about working for a small-to-medium business or ISP. Every effort has been made to make this book as complete and as accurate as possible, but no warranty or fitness is implied.

The information is provided on an "as is" basis. The authors, Cisco Press, and Cisco Systems, Inc. shall have neither liability nor responsibility to any person or entity with respect to any loss or damages arising from the information contained in this book or from the use of the discs or programs that may accompany it.

The opinions expressed in this book belong to the author and are not necessarily those of Cisco Systems, Inc.

Publisher
Paul Boger

Associate Publisher
Dave Dusthimer

Cisco Representative
Erik Ullanderson

Cisco Press Program Manager
Anand Sundaram

Executive Editor
Mary Beth Ray

Managing Editor
Patrick Kanouse

Project Editor
Bethany Wall

Editorial Assistant
Vanessa Evans

Cover Designer
Louisa Adair

Composition
Mark Shirar

Trademark Acknowledgments

All terms mentioned in this book that are known to be trademarks or service marks have been appropriately capitalized. Cisco Press or Cisco Systems, Inc., cannot attest to the accuracy of this information. Use of a term in this book should not be regarded as affecting the validity of any trademark or service mark.

Feedback Information

At Cisco Press, our goal is to create in-depth technical books of the highest quality and value. Each book is crafted with care and precision, undergoing rigorous development that involves the unique expertise of members from the professional technical community.

Readers' feedback is a natural continuation of this process. If you have any comments regarding how we could improve the quality of this book, or otherwise alter it to better suit your needs, you can contact us through email at feedback@ciscopress.com. Please make sure to include the book title and ISBN in your message.

We greatly appreciate your assistance.

Americas Headquarters
Cisco Systems, Inc.
San Jose, CA

Asia Pacific Headquarters
Cisco Systems (USA) Pte. Ltd.
Singapore

Europe Headquarters
Cisco Systems International BV
Amsterdam, The Netherlands

Cisco has more than 200 offices worldwide. Addresses, phone numbers, and fax numbers are listed on the Cisco Website at **www.cisco.com/go/offices.**

CCDE, CCENT, Cisco Eos, Cisco HealthPresence, the Cisco logo, Cisco Lumin, Cisco Nexus, Cisco StadiumVision, Cisco TelePresence, Cisco WebEx, DCE, and Welcome to the Human Network are trademarks; Changing the Way We Work, Live, Play, and Learn and Cisco Store are service marks; and Access Registrar, Aironet, AsyncOS, Bringing the Meeting To You, Catalyst, CCDA, CCDP, CCIE, CCIP, CCNA, CCNP, CCSP, CCVP, Cisco, the Cisco Certified Internetwork Expert logo, Cisco IOS, Cisco Press, Cisco Systems, Cisco Systems Capital, the Cisco Systems logo, Cisco Unity, Collaboration Without Limitation, EtherFast, EtherSwitch, Event Center, Fast Step, Follow Me Browsing, FormShare, GigaDrive, HomeLink, Internet Quotient, IOS, iPhone, iQuick Study, IronPort, the IronPort logo, LightStream, Linksys, MediaTone, MeetingPlace, MeetingPlace Chime Sound, MGX, Networkers, Networking Academy, Network Registrar, PCNow, PIX, PowerPanels, ProConnect, ScriptShare, SenderBase, SMARTnet, Spectrum Expert, StackWise, The Fastest Way to Increase Your Internet Quotient, TransPath, WebEx, and the WebEx logo are registered trademarks of Cisco Systems, Inc. and/or its affiliates in the United States and certain other countries.

All other trademarks mentioned in this document or website are the property of their respective owners. The use of the word partner does not imply a partnership relationship between Cisco and any other company. (0812R)

Contents at a Glance

Contents

Command Syntax Conventions

The conventions used to present command syntax in this book are the same conventions used in the IOS Command Reference. The Command Reference describes these conventions as follows:

- **Boldface** indicates commands and keywords that are entered literally as shown. In actual configuration examples and output (not general command syntax), boldface indicates commands that are manually input by the user (such as a **show** command).

- *Italic* indicates arguments for which you supply actual values.

- Vertical bars (|) separate alternative, mutually exclusive elements.

- Square brackets ([ ]) indicate an optional element.

- Braces ({ }) indicate a required choice.

- Braces within brackets ([{ }]) indicate a required choice within an optional element.

About This Course Booklet

Your Cisco Networking Academy Course Booklet is designed as a study resource you can easily read, highlight, and review on the go, wherever the Internet is not available or practical:

- The text is extracted directly, word-for-word, from the online course so you can highlight important points and take notes in the "Your Chapter Notes" section.

- Headings with the exact page correlations provide a quick reference to the online course for your classroom discussions and exam preparation.

- An icon system directs you to the online curriculum to take full advantage of the images, labs, Packet Tracer activities, and dynamic Flash-based activities embedded within the Networking Academy online course interface.

Refer to **Figure** in online course | Refer to **Lab Activity** for this chapter | Refer to **Packet Tracer Activity** for this chapter | Refer to **Interactive Graphic** in online course. | Go to the online course to take the quiz.

The Course Booklet is a faster, economical paper-based way to help you succeed with the Cisco Networking Academy online course.

Course Introduction

Welcome

Welcome to the CCNA Discovery course, Working at a Small-to-Medium Business or ISP. The goal of this course is to assist you in developing the skills necessary to provide customer support to users of small-to-medium-sized networks and across a range of applications. The course provides an introduction to routing and remote access, addressing and network services. It will also familiarize you with servers providing email services, web space, and Authenticated Access. This course prepares you with the skills required for entry-level Help Desk Technician and entry-level Network Technician jobs.

More than just information

This computer-based learning environment is an important part of the overall course experience for students and instructors in the Networking Academy. These online course materials are designed to be used along with several other instructional tools and activities. These include:

- Class presentation, discussion, and practice with your instructor
- Hands-on labs that use networking equipment within the Networking Academy classroom
- Online scored assessments and grade book
- Packet Tracer 4.1 simulation tool
- Additional software for classroom activities

A global community

When you participate in the Networking Academy, you are joining a global community linked by common goals and technologies. Schools, colleges, universities and other entities in over 160 countries participate in the program. You can see an interactive network map of the global Networking Academy community at http://www.academynetspace.com.

The material in this course encompasses a broad range of technologies that facilitate how people work, live, play, and learn by communicating with voice, video, and other data. Networking and the Internet affect people differently in different parts of the world. Although we have worked with instructors from around the world to create these materials, it is important that you work with your instructor and fellow students to make the material in this course applicable to your local situation.

Keep in Touch

These online instructional materials, as well as the rest of the course tools, are part of the larger Networking Academy. The portal for the program is located at http://cisco.netacad.net. There you will obtain access to the other tools in the program such as the assessment server and student grade book), as well as informational updates and other relevant links.

Mind Wide Open®

An important goal in education is to enrich you, the student, by expanding what you know and can do. It is important to realize, however, that the instructional materials and the instructor can only facilitate the process. You must make the commitment yourself to learn new skills. Below are a few suggestions to help you learn and grow.

1. Take notes. Professionals in the networking field often keep Engineering Journals in which they write down the things they observe and learn. Taking notes is an important way to help your understanding grow over time.

2. Think about it. The course provides information both to change what you know and what you can do. As you go through the course, ask yourself what makes sense and what doesn't. Stop and ask questions when you are confused. Try to find out more about topics that interest you. If you are not sure why something is being taught, consider asking your instructor or a friend. Think about how the different parts of the course fit together.

3. Practice. Learning new skills requires practice. We believe this is so important to e-learning that we have a special name for it. We call it e-doing. It is very important that you complete the activities in the online instructional materials and that you also complete the hands-on labs and Packet Tracer® activities.

4. Practice again. Have you ever thought that you knew how to do something and then, when it was time to show it on a test or at work, you discovered that you really hadn't mastered it? Just like learning any new skill like a sport, game, or language, learning a professional skill requires patience and repeated practice before you can say you have truly learned it. The online instructional materials in this course provide opportunities for repeated practice for many skills. Take full advantage of them. You can also work with your instructor to extend Packet Tracer, and other tools, for additional practice as needed.

5. Teach it. Teaching a friend or colleague is often a good way to reinforce your own learning. To teach well, you will have to work through details that you may have overlooked on your first reading. Conversations about the course material with fellow students, colleagues, and the instructor can help solidify your understanding of networking concepts.

6. Make changes as you go. The course is designed to provide feedback through interactive activities and quizzes, the online assessment system, and through interactions with your instructor. You can use this feedback to better understand where your strengths and weaknesses are. If there is an area that you are having trouble with, focus on studying or practicing more in that area. Seek additional feedback from your instructor and other students.

Explore the world of networking

This version of the course includes a special tool called Packet Tracer 4.1®. Packet Tracer is a networking learning tool that supports a wide range of physical and logical simulations. It also provides visualization tools to help you to understand the internal workings of a network.

The Packet Tracer activities included in the course consist of network simulations, games, activities, and challenges that provide a broad range of learning experiences.

Create your own worlds

You can also use Packet Tracer to create your own experiments and networking scenarios. We hope that, over time, you consider using Packet Tracer – not only for experiencing the activities included in the course, but also to become an author, explorer, and experimenter.

The online course materials have embedded Packet Tracer activities that will launch on computers running Windows® operating systems, if Packet Tracer is installed. This integration may also work on other operating systems using Windows emulation.

CHAPTER 1

The Internet and Its Uses

Introduction

Refer to
Figure
in online course

1.1 What is the Internet?

1.1.1 The Internet and Standards

Refer to
Figure
in online course

The *Internet* is a worldwide, publicly accessible network of networks. It enables individuals and businesses alike, through interconnected computer networks, to share information, resources, and services.

In the beginning, the Internet was used strictly for scientific, educational, and military research. In 1991, regulations changed to allow businesses and consumers to connect as well. The Internet has grown rapidly, and is now global. New technologies are continuously being developed that make the Internet easier and more attractive to use. Online applications are available to the Internet user, including email, web browsing, streaming music and video, gaming, and instant messaging.

The way people interact, share information, and even do business is changing to keep up with the continuous evolution of this global network. The Internet is creating a wider audience and consumer base for whatever message, product, or service can be delivered. For many businesses, having Internet access has become critical, not only for communication but also for day-to-day operation. Some of the business uses of the Internet include:

- *E-Commerce*
- Communications
- Collaboration and training

Refer to
Figure
in online course

With the increasing number of new devices and technologies coming online, how is it possible to manage all the changes and still reliably deliver services such as email? The answer is Internet standards.

A standard is a set of rules that determines how something must be done. Networking and Internet standards ensure that all devices connecting to the network use the same set of rules. Using standards, it is possible for different types of devices to send information to each other over the Internet. For example, the way in which an email is formatted, forwarded, and received by all devices is done according to a standard. If one person sends an email via a personal computer, another person can use a mobile phone to receive and read the email as long as the mobile phone uses the same standards as the personal computer.

An Internet standard is the end result of a comprehensive cycle of discussion, problem solving, and testing. When a new standard is proposed, each stage of the development and approval process is recorded in a numbered Request for Comments (RFC) document so that the evolution of the standard is tracked.

There are thousands of Internet standards that help define the rules for how devices communicate on networks. These different standards are developed, published, and maintained by a variety of different organizations. Because these organizations create and maintain standards, millions of individuals are able to connect to the Internet using a variety of devices, including personal computers, mobile phones, handheld personal digital assistants (PDAs), MP3 players, and even televisions.

1.1.2 ISP and ISP Services

Refer to **Figure** in online course

Regardless of the type of device that an individual or business uses to connect to the Internet, the device must connect through an Internet service provider (*ISP*). An ISP is a company or organization through which a subscriber obtains Internet access. A subscriber can be a business, a private consumer, a government body, or even another ISP.

In addition to offering connection to the Internet, an ISP can offer other services to subscribers, including:

- *Equipment co-location* - A business may opt to have some or all internal network equipment physically located on the ISP premises.

- *Web hosting* - The ISP provides the server and application software for storing web pages and web content for the business website.

- *FTP* - The ISP provides the server and application software for the *FTP* site of a business.

- *Applications and media hosting* - The ISP provides the server and software to allow a business to provide *stream*ing media such as music, video, or applications such as online databases.

- *Voice over IP* - A business can save on long distance telephone charges, especially for internal calls between geographically distant offices, by using Voice over IP (VoIP).

- *Technical support* - Many businesses do not have the in-house technical expertise to manage large internal networks. Some ISPs provide technical support and consulting services for an additional fee.

- *Point of Presence (POP)* - A business has the option of connecting to the ISP through POP, using a variety of access technologies.

Refer to **Interactive Graphic** in online course.

Activity

Match the requirements of an end user to various ISPs.

After reading the scenario, place a check in the box that is the most appropriate ISP for each user.

1.2 ISPs

1.2.1 Delivering Internet Services to End Users

Refer to
Figure
in online course

To gain access to the Internet, it is first necessary to have a connection to an ISP. ISPs offer various connection options. The main connection methods used by home and small business users are:

Dialup access

Dialup access is an inexpensive option that uses any phone line and a modem. To connect to the ISP, a user calls the ISP access phone number. Dialup is the slowest connection option, and is typically used by mobile workers and in areas where higher speed connection options are not available.

DSL

Digital subscriber line, or *DSL*, is more expensive than dialup, but provides a faster connection. DSL also uses telephone lines, but unlike dialup access, DSL provides a continuous connection to the Internet. This connection option uses a special high-speed modem that separates the DSL signal from the telephone signal and provides an Ethernet connection to a host computer or *LAN*.

Cable modem

A *cable modem* is a connection option offered by cable television service providers. The Internet signal is carried on the same coaxial cable that delivers cable television to homes and businesses. A special cable modem separates the Internet signal from the other signals carried on the cable and provides an Ethernet connection to a host computer or LAN.

Satellite

Satellite connection is an option offered by satellite service providers. The user's computer connects through Ethernet to a satellite modem that transmits radio signals to the nearest Point of Presence, or POP, within the satellite network.

Refer to
Figure
in online course

Bandwidth is measured in bits per second (bps). Higher bandwidth speeds are measured in kilobits per second (kbps), megabits per second (Mbps), or gigabits per second (Gbps).

There are three main types of high-bandwidth connection options that are used by businesses:

- **T1 connections** transmit data up to 1.544 Mbps. T1 connections are symmetrical, meaning that the upload bandwidth is the same as the download bandwidth. A medium-sized business may need only one T1 connection. E1 is a European standard that transmits data at 2.048 Mbps.

- *T3 connection*s transmit data up to 45 Mbps. Although considerably more expensive than a T1 connection, larger businesses may need a T3 connection to accommodate the number of employees. Large businesses with multiple locations might use a combination of T1 and T3 lines. E3 is a European standard that transmits data at 34.368 Mbps.

- *Metro Ethernet* offers a wide range of high-bandwidth options, including Gbps links. Large companies with many branches in the same city, such as banks, use Metro Ethernet. Metro Ethernet connects the main office location and all the branches using switched technology. Metro Ethernet allows the transfer of large amounts of data faster and less expensively than other high-bandwidth connection options.

Refer to
Figure
in online course

After the type of connection is established, it is necessary to connect to the ISP to get access to the Internet. Individual computers and business networks connect to the ISP at the POP. POPs are located at the edge of the ISP network and serve a particular geographical region. They provide a local point of connection and *authentication* (password control) for multiple end users. An ISP may have many POPs, depending on the size of the POP and the area that it services.

Within the ISP network, high-speed routers and switches move data between the various POPs. Multiple links interconnect the POPs to provide alternate routes in case one of the links becomes overloaded with *traffic* or fails.

1.2.2 Internet Hierarchy

Refer to
Figure
in online course

The Internet has a hierarchical structure. At the top of this *hierarchy* are the ISP organizations. The ISP POPs connect to an Internet Exchange Point (IXP). In some countries, this is called a Network Access Point (*NAP*). An IXP or NAP is where multiple ISPs join together to gain access to each other's networks and exchange information. There are currently over 100 major exchange points located worldwide.

The Internet backbone consists of this group of networks owned by various organizations and interconnected through IXPs and *private peer*ing connections.

The Internet backbone is like an information super highway that provides high-speed data links to interconnect the POPs and IXPs in major metropolitan areas around the world. The primary *medium* that connects the Internet backbone is fiber-optic cable. This cable is typically installed underground to connect cities within continents. Fiber-optic cables also run under the sea to connect continents, countries, and cities.

Refer to
Figure
in online course

ISPs are classified into different tiers according to how they access the Internet backbone:

- *Tier 1* ISPs are the top of the hierarchy. Tier 1 ISPs are huge organizations that connect directly with each other through private peering, physically joining their individual network backbones together to create the global Internet backbone. Within their own networks, the Tier 1 ISPs own the routers, high-speed data links, and other pieces of equipment that join them to other Tier 1 ISP networks. This includes the undersea cables that connect the continents.

- *Tier 2* ISPs are the next tier in terms of backbone access. Tier 2 ISPs can also be very large, even extending across several countries, but very few have networks that span entire continents or between continents. To provide their customers with global Internet access, some Tier 2 ISPs pay Tier 1 ISPs to carry their traffic to other parts of the world. Some Tier 2 ISPs exchange global traffic with other ISPs less expensively through *public peer*ing at IXPs. A large IXP may bring together hundreds of ISPs in a central physical location for access to multiple networks over a shared connection.

- *Tier 3* ISPs are the farthest away from the backbone. Tier 3 ISPs are generally found in major cities and provide customers local access to the Internet. Tier 3 ISPs pay Tier 1 and 2 ISPs for access to the global Internet and Internet services.

1.2.3 Using Tools to Map the Internet

Refer to
Figure
in online course

Network utilities create a map of the various interconnections to visualize how ISP networks interconnect. These utilities also illustrate the speed at which each connecting point can be reached.

The `ping` command tests the accessibility of a specific *IP address*. The `ping` command sends an *ICMP* (Internet Control Message Protocol) echo request *packet* to the destination address and then waits for an echo reply packet to return from that host. ICMP is an Internet protocol that is used to verify communications. It measures the time that elapses between when the request packet is sent and the response packet is received. The `ping` command output indicates whether the reply was received successfully and displays the round-trip time for the transmissions.

To use the `ping` command, enter the following command at the Cisco command line interface (CLI) router prompt or at the Windows command prompt:

`ping <ip address>`

where `<ip address>` is the IP address of the destination device.

Refer to
Figure
in online course

For example, `ping 192.168.30.1`.

If a packet does not reach the destination, or if delays are encountered along the way, how is it determined where the problem is located or through which routers the packet has passed?

The `traceroute` utility displays the path that a packet takes from the source to the destination host. Each router that the packet passes through is called a *hop*. Traceroute displays each hop along the way. It also calculates the time between when the packet is sent and when a reply is received from the router at each hop.

If a problem occurs, use the output of the `traceroute` utility to help determine where a packet was lost or delayed. The output also shows the various ISP organizations that the packet must pass through during its journey from source to destination.

The Windows `tracert` utility works the same way. There are also a number of visual `traceroute` programs that provide a graphical display of the route that a packet takes.

Refer to
Lab Activity
for this chapter

Lab Activity

Use `traceroute` to check ISP connectivity through the Internet.

Refer to **Packet
Tracer Activity**
for this chapter

Packet Tracer Activity

Interpret the output of `ping` and `traceroute`.

1.3 ISP Connectivity

1.3.1 ISP Requirements

Refer to
Figure
in online course

An ISP requires a variety of devices to accept input from end users and provide services. To participate in a transport network, the ISP must be able to connect to other ISPs. An ISP must also be able to handle large volumes of traffic.

Some of the devices required to provide services include:

- Access devices that enable end users to connect to the ISP, such as a DSL Access Multiplexer (DSLAM) for DSL connections, a Cable Modem Termination System (*CMTS*) for cable connections, modems for dialup connections, or wireless bridging equipment for wireless access.

- Border gateway routers to enable the ISP to connect and transfer data to other ISPs, IXPs, or large business *enterprise* customers.

- Servers for such things as email, network address assignment, web space, FTP hosting, and multimedia hosting.

- Power conditioning equipment with substantial battery backup to maintain continuity if the main power grid fails.

- High capacity air conditioning units to maintain controlled temperatures.

Refer to
Figure
in online course

ISPs, like other businesses, want to expand so that they can increase their income. The ability to expand their business depends on gaining new subscribers and selling more services. However, as the number of subscribers grows, the traffic on the network of the ISP also grows.

Eventually, the increased traffic may overload the network, causing router errors, lost packets, and excessive delays. In an overloaded network, subscribers can wait for minutes for a web page to load, or may even lose network connection. These customers may choose to switch to a competing ISP to get better performance.

Loss of customers directly translates to loss of income for an ISP. For this reason, it is important that the ISP provides a *reliable* and scalable network.

Scalability is the capacity of a network to allow for future change and growth. Scalable networks can expand quickly to support new users and applications without affecting the performance of the service being delivered to existing users.

The most scalable devices are those that are modular and provide expansion slots for adding modules. Different modules can have different numbers of ports. In the case of a chassis router, some modules also offer different interface options, allowing for different connection options on the same chassis.

Refer to Packet Tracer Activity for this chapter

Packet Tracer Activity

Identify appropriate equipment to meet the business needs of ISP customers.

View printable instructions.

1.3.2 Roles and Responsibilities within an ISP

Refer to Figure in online course

ISP organizations consist of many teams and departments which are responsible for ensuring that the network operates smoothly and that the services are available.

Network support services are involved in all aspects of network management, including planning and provisioning of new equipment and circuits, adding new subscribers, network repair and maintenance, and customer service for network *connectivity* issues.

When a new business subscriber orders ISP services, the various network support service teams work together to ensure that the order is processed correctly and that the network is ready to deliver those services as quickly as possible.

Refer to Figure in online course

Each of the network support service teams have their own roles and responsibilities:

- **Customer Service** receives the order from the customer and ensures that the specified requirements of the customer are accurately entered into the order tracking database.

- **Planning and Provisioning** determines whether the new customer has existing network hardware and circuits and if new circuits need to be installed.

- The **On-site Installation** is advised of which circuits and equipment to use and then installs them at the customer site.

- The **Network Operations Center (NOC)** monitors and tests the new connection and ensures that it is performing properly.

- The **Help Desk** is notified by the NOC when the circuit is ready for operation and then contacts the customer to guide them through the process of setting up passwords and other necessary account information.

Refer to Interactive Graphic in online course.

Activity

Match the role to its description.

Drag the role to its defined description.

Chapter Summary

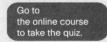

Chapter Quiz

Take the chapter quiz to check your knowledge.

Your Chapter Notes

CHAPTER 2

Help Desk

Introduction

Refer to
Figure
in online course

2.1 Help Desk Technicians

Refer to
Figure
in online course

2.1.1 ISP Help Desk Organization

Many business operations depend on the connection to the local network and to the Internet. Because of this, solving network problems is a top priority for businesses.

ISPs provide the Internet connection for businesses, and they provide their customers support for problems that occur with Internet connectivity. This support usually includes assistance with customer equipment problems. ISP support is typically provided through the ISP help desk. Whether the problem is connecting to the Internet or getting email, the ISP help desk is usually the first place a user or business turns to for help.

ISP help desk technicians have the knowledge and experience to fix problems and get users connected. ISP help desk technicians provide solutions to customer problems with the goal of network optimization and customer retention.

A good help desk team ensures that problems are resolved quickly and to the satisfaction of the customer. Providing Internet services is a highly competitive business, and poor service can cause the ISP to lose customers to competing ISPs.

Refer to
Figure
in online course

At an ISP, there are usually three levels of customer support:

- Level 1 is for immediate support handled by junior-level help desk technicians.

- Level 2 handles calls that are escalated to more experienced telephone support.

- Level 3 is for calls that cannot be resolved by phone support and require a visit by an on-site technician.

In addition to ISPs, many other types of medium to large businesses employ help desk or customer support teams. The titles assigned to the technicians may vary from those described here, although the three-level hierarchy is the most common structure. Depending on the size of the organization, the help desk can consist of one person that performs all three levels of support, or it can be a comprehensive call center with elaborate call routing facilities and escalation rules. Some ISPs and businesses contract out their help desk functions to a third-party call center company, which provides the services of Level 1 and Level 2 technicians.

2.1.2 Roles of ISP Technicians

Refer to
Figure
in online course

When a user initially contacts the help desk to resolve an issue, the call or message is usually directed to a Level 1 support technician. Level 1 support is usually an entry-level position that provides junior technicians with valuable experience. Many customer issues are resolved by the Level 1 support technician.

Issues that cannot be resolved are sent to Level 2 support, which typically has fewer agents available. The duties and responsibilities of the Level 2 technician are similar to that of the Level 1 technician, but they are at a higher skill level. These agents are expected to solve problems that are more challenging and require more knowledge.

Refer to
Figure
in online course

Many larger service providers have expanded their businesses to include *managed services* or on-site support of a customer network. Organizations that provide managed services are sometimes referred to as Managed Service Providers (MSP). Managed services can be provided by ISPs, telecommunications service providers, or other types of computer and network support organizations. When an ISP is providing managed services, it often requires technicians to visit customer sites for the purpose of installation and support. This type of service represents Level 3 support.

Level 3 support is usually in accordance with a Service Level Agreement (*SLA*). An SLA resembles an insurance policy, because it provides coverage or service if there is a computer or network problem.

Refer to
Interactive Graphic
in online course.

Activity

Identify the responsibilities of each level of network technician.

For each task, select the appropriate technician.

2.1.3 Interacting with Customers

Refer to
Figure
in online course

Help desk technicians may be required to provide phone support, email support, web-based support, online chat support, and possibly on-site support. They are often the first point of contact for frustrated and anxious customers. Until a problem is solved, help desk technicians may continue to get calls and correspondence asking for status updates and time estimates to resolve an issue.

The help desk technician must be able to stay focused in an environment with frequent interruptions and perform multiple tasks efficiently and accurately. It can be difficult to consistently maintain a positive attitude and provide a high level of service. The help desk technician has to have excellent interpersonal skills and effective communication skills, both oral and written. The technician must be able to work independently and as part of a team.

It is important for the help desk technician to be able to handle customer issues with speed, efficiency, and professionalism. Help desk technicians should conduct themselves in accordance with the company's customer service philosophy. A customer service philosophy is an organization-wide ethic shared by everyone from top management to operational staff.

Basic *incident management* procedures must be followed every time a help desk technician receives a call and begins troubleshooting issues. Incident management includes opening a trouble ticket and following a problem-solving strategy. Problem-solving techniques include using troubleshooting flowcharts, addressing questions in a template format, and maintaining proper ticket escalation procedures.

A help desk script is used by the help desk technician to gather information and cover the important facts about customer incident.

Refer to
Figure
in online course

In addition to technical ability, help desk technicians must be able to greet customers pleasantly and be professional and courteous throughout the call.

Customer service and interpersonal skills are especially important when handling difficult clients and incidents. The help desk technician must know how to relieve customer stress and respond to abusive customers.

Opening trouble tickets and logging information on the tickets are critical to help desk operation. When there are many calls relating to a single problem or symptom, it is helpful to have information on how the problem was resolved in the past. It is also important to relay to the customer what is being done to solve the problem. Good information on open trouble tickets helps communicate accurate status, both to the customer and other ISP personnel.

Refer to
Figure
in online course

While many issues can be handled remotely, some problems require an on-site visit to the customer premises to install and troubleshoot equipment. When a technician goes on-site, it is important to represent their organization in a professional manner. A professional knows how to make the customer feel at ease and confident in the technician's skills.

On the first visit to a customer location, it is important for the technician to make a good impression. Personal grooming and the way the technician is dressed are the first things the customer notices. If the technician makes a bad first impression, it may be difficult to change that impression and gain the confidence of the customer. Many employers provide a uniform or have a dress code for their on-site technicians.

The language and attitude of the technician also reflect on the organization that the technician represents. A customer may be anxious or concerned about how the new equipment will operate. When speaking with a customer, the technician should be polite and respectful, and answer all customer questions. If the technician does not know an answer to a customer question or if additional information is required, the technician should write down the customer inquiry and follow up on it as soon as possible.

Refer to
Interactive Graphic
in online course.

Activity

Examine each statement and decide to which part of the customer support process it belongs.

For each statement, select the appropriate item.

2.2 OSI Model

2.2.1 Using the OSI Model

Refer to
Figure
in online course

When a network connectivity problem is reported to the help desk, many methods are available to diagnose the problem. One common method is to troubleshoot the problem using a layered approach. A layered approach requires that the network technician be familiar with the various functions that occur as messages are created, delivered, and interpreted by the network devices and hosts on the network.

Moving data across a network is best visualized using the seven layers of the Open Systems Interconnection model, commonly referred to as the OSI model. The OSI model breaks network communications down into multiple processes. Each process is a small part of the larger task.

For example, in a vehicle manufacturing plant, the entire vehicle is not assembled by one person. Rather the vehicle moves from station to station where specialized teams add specific components. The complex task of assembling a vehicle is made easier by breaking it into manageable and logical tasks. This process also makes troubleshooting easier. When a problem occurs in the manufacturing process, it is possible to isolate the problem to the specific task where the defect was introduced, and then fix it.

In a similar manner, the OSI model can be used as a means to focus on a layer when troubleshooting to identify and resolve network problems.

Refer to
Figure
in online course

The seven layers of the OSI model are divided into two parts: upper layers and lower layers.

The term upper layer is sometimes used to refer to any layer above the Transport layer of the OSI model. The upper layers deal with application functionality and are generally implemented only in software. The highest layer, the *Application layer*, is closest to the end user.

The term lower layer is sometimes used to refer to any layer below the Session layer. The combined functionality of the lower layers handles data transport. The Physical layer and the Data Link layer are implemented in both hardware and software. The Physical layer is closest to the physical network medium, or network cabling. The Physical layer actually places information on the medium.

End stations, like clients and servers, usually work with all seven layers. Networking devices are only concerned with the lower layers. Hubs work on Layer 1, switches on Layers 1 and 2, routers on Layers 1, 2 and 3, and firewalls on Layers 1, 2, 3, and 4.

2.2.2 OSI Model Protocols and Technologies

Refer to
Figure
in online course

When using the OSI model as a framework for troubleshooting, it is important to understand which functions are performed at each layer, and what network information is available to the devices or software programs performing these functions. For example, many processes must occur for email to successfully travel from the client to the server. The OSI model divides the task of sending and receiving email into smaller, distinct steps that correspond with the seven layers.

Step 1: Upper layers create the data.

When a user sends an email message, the *alphanumeric character*s within the message are converted to data that can travel across the network. Layers 7, 6, and 5 are responsible for ensuring that the message is placed in a format that can be understood by the application running on the destination host. This process is called *encoding*. The upper layers then send the encoded messages to the lower layers for transport across the network. Transporting the email to the correct server relies on the configuration information provided by the user. Problems that occur at the application layer are often related to errors in the configuration of the user software programs.

Refer to
Figure
in online course

Step 2: Layer 4 packages the data for end-to-end transport.

The data that comprises the email message is packaged for network transport at Layer 4. Layer 4 breaks the message down into smaller segments. A header is placed on each *segment* indicating the *TCP* or *UDP port number* that corresponds to the correct application layer application. Functions in the transport layer indicate the type of delivery service. Email utilizes TCP segments, therefore packet delivery is acknowledged by the destination. Layer 4 functions are implemented in software that runs on the source and destination hosts. However, because firewalls often use the TCP and UDP port numbers to filter traffic, problems that occur at Layer 4 can be caused by improperly configured firewall filter lists.

Step 3: Layer 3 adds the network IP address information.

The email data received from the transport layer is put into a packet that contains a header with the source and destination network IP addresses. Routers use the destination address to direct the packets across the network along the appropriate path. Incorrectly configured IP address information on the source or destination system can cause Layer 3 problems to occur. Because routers also use IP address information, router configuration errors can cause problems at this layer.

Refer to
Figure
in online course

Step 4: Layer 2 adds the data link layer header and trailer.

Each network device in the path from the source to the destination, including the sending host, encapsulates the packet into a frame. The frame contains the physical address of the next directly-connected network device on the link. Each device in the chosen network path requires framing so that it can connect to the next device. Switches and network interface cards (NICs) use the information in the frame to deliver the message to the correct destination device. Incorrect NIC drivers, interface cards, and hardware problems with switches can cause Layer 2 problems to occur.

Step 5: Layer 1 converts the data to bits for transmission.

The frame is converted into a pattern of 1s and 0s (bits) for transmission on the medium. A clocking function enables the devices to distinguish these bits as they travel across the medium. The medium can change along the path between the source and destination. For example, the email message can originate on an Ethernet LAN, cross a fiber campus backbone, and cross a serial *WAN* link until it reaches its destination on another remote Ethernet LAN. Layer 1 problems can be caused by loose or incorrect cables, malfunctioning interface cards, or electrical interference.

At the receiving host, the processes described in steps 1 through 5 are reversed, with the message traveling back up the layers to the appropriate application.

Refer to
Interactive Graphic
in online course.

Activity

Identify the layer to which the protocol or technology belongs.

For each protocol or technology displayed, click the appropriate layer.

2.2.3 Troubleshooting the OSI Model

Refer to
Figure
in online course

As a theoretical model, the OSI model defines the protocols, hardware, and other specifications that operate at the seven layers.

The OSI model also provides a systematic basis for troubleshooting a network. In any troubleshooting scenario, the basic problem-solving procedure includes the following steps:

1. Define the problem.

2. Isolate the cause of the problem.

3. Solve the problem.

- Identify and prioritize alternative solutions.

- Select one alternative as the solution.

- Implement the solution.

- Evaluate the solution.

If an identified solution does not fix the problem, undo any changes and proceed to the next possible solution. Go through the steps until a solution works.

In addition to the basic problem-solving procedures, the OSI model can be used as a guideline for troubleshooting. Using a layered model, there are three different troubleshooting approaches that a technician can use to isolate the problem:

- *Bottom-Up -* The bottom-up approach starts with the physical components of the network and works its way up the layers of the OSI model. Bottom-up troubleshooting is an effective and efficient approach for suspected physical problems.

■ *Top-Down* - The top-down approach starts with the user application and works its way down the layers of the OSI model. This approach starts with the assumption that the problem is with the application and not the network infrastructure.

■ *Divide-and-Conquer* - The divide-and-conquer approach is generally used by more experienced network technicians. The technician makes an educated guess targeting the problem layer and then based on the observed results, moves up or down the OSI layers.

Using the OSI model as a guide, the help desk technician can query the customer to help define the problem and isolate the cause.

Refer to
Figure
in online course

The help desk technician usually has a standard checklist or script to follow when troubleshooting a problem. Often the script takes a bottom-up approach to troubleshooting. This is because physical problems are usually the simplest to diagnose and repair, and the bottom-up approach starts with the Physical Layer.

Layer 1 Troubleshooting

The technician starts with Layer 1 issues first. Remember, Layer 1 deals with the physical connectivity of the network devices. Layer 1 problems often involve cabling and electricity, and are the reasons for many help desk calls. Some of the more common Layer 1 problems include:

■ Device power turned off

■ Device power unplugged

■ Loose network cable connection

■ Incorrect cable type

■ Faulty network cable

■ Faulty wireless access point

■ Incorrect wireless settings, such as the SSID

To troubleshoot at Layer 1, first check that all devices have the proper electrical supply, and that the devices are turned on. This may seem to be an obvious solution, but many times the person reporting the problem may overlook a device that is within the network path from source to destination. If there are any LEDs that display the status of the connectivity, verify with the customer that they are indicating correctly. If on-site, visually inspect all network cabling and reconnect cables to ensure a proper connection. If the problem is with wireless, verify that the wireless access point is operational and that wireless settings are configured correctly.

When remotely troubleshooting a problem, the technician should advise the caller through each step, what to look for, and what to do if an error is found. If it is determined that all Layer 1 issues have been addressed, it is time to travel up the OSI model to Layer 2.

Refer to
Figure
in online course

Layer 2 Troubleshooting

Network switches and host NICs perform Layer 2 functions. Layer 2 problems can be caused by faulty equipment, incorrect device drivers, or an improperly configured switch. When remotely troubleshooting a problem, it may be difficult to isolate a Layer 2 problem.

An on-site technician can check whether the NIC is installed and working properly. Reseating the NIC, or replacing a suspected faulty NIC with a known good NIC, helps to isolate the problem. The same process can be done with any network switch.

Layer 3 Troubleshooting

At Layer 3, the technician needs to investigate the logical addressing used in the network, such as the IP address scheme. If the network is using IP addressing, the technician verifies that the device has the proper settings, such as:

- IP address within the assigned network

- Correct *subnet mask*

- Correct default gateway

- Other settings as required, such as *DHCP* or DNS

At Layer 3, several utilities can assist with the troubleshooting process. Three of the most common command line tools are:

`ipconfig` - Shows IP settings on the computer

`ping` - Tests basic network connectivity

`tracert` - Determines if the routing path between the source and destination is available

Most network problems can usually be resolved using these Layer 1, 2, and 3 troubleshooting techniques.

Refer to **Figure** in online course

Layer 4 Troubleshooting

If Layers 1 through 3 all appear to be operating normally and the technician can successfully `ping` the IP address of the remote server, it is time to check the higher layers. For example, if a network firewall is used along the path, it is important to check that the application TCP or UDP port is open and no filter lists are blocking traffic to that port.

Layers 5 through 7 Troubleshooting

The technician should also check the application configuration. For example, if troubleshooting an email issue, ensure that the application is configured with the correct sending and receiving email server information. It is also necessary to ensure that domain name resolution is functioning as expected.

For remote technicians, higher layer issues can be checked by using other network utility tools, such as a packet sniffer, to view traffic as it crosses the network. A network application, such as Telnet, can also be used to view configurations.

Refer to **Interactive Graphic** in online course.

Activity

Identify if a network issue is occurring at Layer 1, Layer 2, Layer 3, Layer 4, or Layers 5 through 7.

Based on the scenario, check the appropriate layer.

2.3 ISP Troubleshooting

2.3.1 Help Desk Troubleshooting Scenarios

Refer to **Figure** in online course

The number and types of calls received by the help desk can vary extensively. Some of the most common calls include problems with email, host configuration, and connectivity.

Email Issues

- Can receive but not send

- Can send but not receive

- Cannot send or receive

- Nobody can reply to messages

A common cause of many email problems is using the wrong POP, *IMAP*, or *SMTP* server names. It is best to check with the email administrator to confirm the proper name of the POP or IMAP server and SMTP server. In some cases, the same server name for both POP/IMAP and SMTP are used. Also, confirm that the username and password are correct. Since the password is not usually displayed, it is a good idea to carefully re-enter it.

When troubleshooting these issues over the phone, it is important to step the customer through the configuration parameters carefully. Many customers are unfamiliar with the terminology and the settings of the various configuration parameters. If possible, connect to the customer device via remote management software. This allows the technician to perform the necessary steps for the customer.

Refer to **Figure** in online course

Host Configuration Issues

A common issue that can prevent connectivity to the Internet or other network resources is improperly configured host addressing information. This can include an incorrect IP address, subnet mask, or default gateway.

In environments where the IP addressing information is manually configured, it is possible that the IP configuration was simply entered incorrectly. In environments where hosts are configured to dynamically receive an IP address from an assignment server, such as a DHCP server, the server may fail or become unreachable due to network issues.

If a host is configured to receive an address dynamically, and an assignment server is unavailable or unreachable, a *link-local address* will be automatically assigned to the local host by the operating system. IPv4 addresses in the address block 169.254.0.1 to 169.254.255.254 (169.254.0.0 /16) are designated as link-local addresses. A link-local process will randomly select an IP address within the 169.254.0.0/16 range. But what prevents two hosts from randomly selecting the same IP address?

Once the link-local process selects an IP address, it sends an *ARP* query with that IP onto the network to see if any other devices are using that address. If there is no response, the IP address is assigned to the device, otherwise another IP address is selected, and the ARP query is repeated. Microsoft refers to link-local addresses as Automatic Private IP Addressing (APIPA).

If multiple hosts on the same network obtain a link-local address, client/server and peer-to-peer applications between those hosts will work properly. However, because link-local addresses are in the private Class B address space, communication outside of the local network is not possible.

When troubleshooting both manually and dynamically configured hosts, use the host command `ipconfig /all` to verify that the host is using the appropriate IP configuration.

Refer to **Figure** in online course

Customer Connectivity Issues

Connectivity problems are more common with new customers trying to connect for the first time. However, sometimes existing customers encounter connectivity issues. First-time customers may have problems with installing the hardware as well as software configuration settings. Existing customers notice connectivity problems when they cannot open a web page or connect to instant messaging or email.

There are many reasons why a customer has no connectivity, including the following:

- Delinquent payments for services

- Hardware failures

- Physical layer failures

- Incorrect application settings

- Missing application plug-ins

- Missing applications

In many cases, the problem is simply a faulty cable, or a cable plugged into an incorrect port. These types of issues can be resolved by checking the cable connection or replacing the cable.

Other problems, such as software issues, may be more difficult to detect. One example is an incorrectly loaded *TCP/IP stack*, preventing IP from operating correctly. The TCP/IP stack can be tested and verified using a loopback address. The loopback is a special address, the reserved IPv4 address 127.0.0.1, which hosts use to direct traffic to themselves. The loopback address creates a shortcut method for TCP/IP applications and services that run on the same device to communicate.

You can ping the loopback address to test the configuration of TCP/IP on the local host. If you are unable to get a response when pinging the loopback address, suspect an improperly configured or installed TCP/IP stack.

Addresses 127.0.0.0 through 127.255.255.255 are reserved for testing purposes. Any address within this block will loop back within the local host. No address within this block should ever appear on any network. Despite the fact that the entire 127.0.0.0/8 network range is reserved, the only address typically used for loopback testing is the 127.0.0.1 address.

Refer to **Packet Tracer Activity** for this chapter

Packet Tracer Activity

Troubleshoot and resolve a network connectivity issue.

2.3.2 Creating and Using Help Desk Records

Refer to **Figure** in online course

When a Level 1 help desk technician receives a call, there is a process followed to gather information. There are also specific systems for storing and retrieving relevant information. It is extremely important to gather the information correctly in the event that a call has to be escalated to Layer 2 or require an on-site visit.

The information gathering and recording process starts as soon as the technician answers the phone. When the customer identifies who they are, the technician accesses the relevant customer information. Typically, a database application is used to manage the customer information.

The information is transferred to a trouble ticket, or incident report. This document can be a piece of paper in a paper filing system or an electronic tracking system designed to follow the troubleshooting process from beginning to end. Each person who works on the problem is expected to record what was done on the trouble ticket. When an on-site call is required, the trouble ticket information can be converted to a work order that the on-site technician can take to the customer site.

When a problem is resolved, the solution is documented in the customer work order or trouble ticket, and in a knowledge-base document for future reference.

Occasionally, the Level 1help desk technician may receive a call that cannot be resolved quickly. In this instance, the technician is responsible for passing the call to a Level 2 technician who is more qualified to resolve the issue. Passing the call to a higher level technician is known as the call escalation process.

Both Level 1 and Level 2 help desk technicians attempt to solve customer problems using the telephone, web tools, and possibly remote desktop sharing applications.

Refer to
Figure
in online course

If the help desk technicians are not able to fix the problem remotely, it is often necessary to send a Level 3 on-site technician to the customer premise location. It is the job of the on-site technician to visit the customer premise to physically work on the problem equipment. The help desk technician can make an appointment with the customer for the on-site technician to perform the repairs, or it may be the responsibility of the on-site technician to arrange the appointment.

To properly troubleshoot the problem, the on-site technician reviews the trouble ticket to see what was previously done. This review gives the technician some background information and a logical starting point. It also helps the technician decide which tools and supplies to bring, rather than having to leave the customer site to obtain supplies.

On-site technicians typically work on the network at the customer location, although there are instances where the technician is unable to make the needed repairs and must bring the damaged equipment back to the ISP site for additional troubleshooting.

2.3.3 Customer Site Procedures

Refer to
Figure
in online course

There are four steps an on-site technician performs before beginning any troubleshooting or repair at the customer site:

Step 1. Provide proper identification to the customer.

Step 2. Review the trouble ticket or work order with the customer to verify that the information is correct.

Step 3. Communicate the current status of any identified problems and the actions the technician expects to take at the customer site that day.

Step 4. Obtain permission from the customer to begin the work.

The technician must verify all items on the trouble ticket. Once the technician is familiar with all issues, the work can begin. The technician is responsible for checking all device and network settings, and running any necessary utilities. The technician may also have to swap out suspected faulty hardware with known good hardware to determine if a hardware problem exists.

Refer to
Figure
in online course

When performing any troubleshooting tasks the customer site, especially when installing new or replacing existing equipment, it is important to minimize the risk of injury by following good safety practices. Many employers offer safety training as part of their employee services.

Ladders

Use ladders to reach high locations to install networking cable and to install or troubleshoot wireless access points in places that are difficult to reach. To reduce the risk of falling off the ladder or dropping equipment while climbing on the ladder, work with a partner whenever possible.

High or Dangerous Locations

Sometimes network equipment and cables are located in high and dangerous places, such as on the side of a building, on roof tops, or in an internal structure such as an elevator shaft, that is not accessible by a ladder. Work performed at this type of location must be done very carefully. Using a safety harness reduces the risk of falling.

Electrical Equipment

If there is a risk of damaging or coming in contact with any electrical lines when handling hardware, consult with the electrician of the customer about measures that can be taken to reduce the risk of electrical shock. Coming in contact with electrical equipment may result in serious personal injury.

Awkward Spaces

Network equipment is often located in narrow and awkward spaces. Ensure that the work area is properly lighted and ventilated. Determine the best way to lift, install, and remove equipment to minimize the risks.

Heavy Equipment

Networking devices can be large and heavy. Plan to have the correct equipment and trained personnel when heavy equipment needs to be installed or moved at a customer site.

Refer to **Figure** in online course

After the technician makes any configuration changes or installs new equipment, the technician must observe the results to ensure proper operation. When finished, the technician communicates the nature of the identified problem to the customer, what solution was applied, and any follow-up procedures. Before the problem can be considered fully resolved, the technician must obtain the acceptance of the customer. The technician can then close the trouble ticket and document the solution.

A copy of the documentation is left with the customer. The document includes the original help desk call problem and the actions taken to solve the problem. The technician records the solution, and the customer acceptance is indicated on the trouble ticket. For future reference, the technician also records the problem and the solution in the help desk documentation and FAQs.

In some cases, an on-site technician can uncover network problems that require upgrades or reconfiguration of the network devices. When this occurs, it may be outside of the scope of the original trouble ticket. These issues are usually communicated to both the customer and the ISP network personnel for further action.

Chapter Summary

Click through the buttons for summary information.

Chapter Quiz

Go to
the online course
to take the quiz.

Take the chapter quiz to check your knowledge.

Your Chapter Notes

CHAPTER 3

Planning a Network Upgrade

Introduction

Refer to
Figure
in online course

3.1 Documenting the Existing Network

Refer to
Figure
in online course

3.1.1 Site Survey

When a small company grows rapidly, the original network that supports the company often cannot keep pace with the expansion. Employees at the company may not realize how important it is to plan for network upgrades. The business may just add network hardware devices of varying quality from different manufacturers and different network connection technologies to connect new users. The quality of the current network may become degraded as each new user is added, until it can no longer support the level of network traffic that the users generate.

When the network starts to fail, most small businesses look for help to redesign the network to meet the new demands. An ISP or managed service provider may be called in to provide advice, and to install and maintain the network upgrade.

Before a network upgrade can be properly designed, an on-site technician is dispatched to perform a site survey to document the existing network structure. It is also necessary to investigate and document the physical layout of the premises to determine where new equipment can be installed.

Refer to
Figure
in online course

A site survey provides the network designer important information and creates a proper starting point for the project. It shows what is already on site, and gives a good indication as to what is needed.

Important pieces of information that can be gathered during a site survey include:

- Number of users and types of equipment
- Projected growth
- Current Internet connectivity
- Application requirements
- Existing network infrastructure and physical layout
- New services required
- Security and privacy considerations
- Reliability and uptime expectations
- Budget constraints

It is a good idea to obtain a floor plan, if possible. If a floor plan is not available, the technician can draw a diagram indicating the size and location of all rooms. An inventory of existing network hardware and software is also useful to provide a baseline of requirements for the upgrade.

A sales representative may also accompany the technician to the site to interview the customer. The sales representative may ask a series of questions to gather information about the network upgrade needs of the business.

Refer to
Figure
in online course

The technician should be prepared for anything when doing the site survey. Networks do not always meet local codes of practice in terms of electrical, building, or safety regulations, nor adhere to any standards.

Sometimes networks grow haphazardly over time and end up being a mixture of technologies and protocols. The technician should be careful not to offend the customer by expressing an opinion about the quality of the existing installed network.

When visiting the customer premises, the technician should do a thorough overview of the network and computer setup. There may be some obvious issues such as unlabeled cables, poor physical security for network devices, lack of emergency power, or lack of an uninterruptible power supply (UPS) for critical devices. These conditions are noted in the site survey report, in addition to the other requirements gathered from the survey and the customer interview.

When the site survey is completed, it is important that the technician review the results with the customer to ensure that nothing is missed and that there are no errors. If everything is accurate, the site survey provides an excellent basis for the new network design.

3.1.2 Physical and Logical Topologies

Refer to
Figure
in online course

Both the physical and logical topology of the network must be documented. A physical topology is the actual physical location of cables, computers, and other peripherals. A logical topology documents the path that data takes through the network and where network functions, like routing, occur. A technician gathers this information during the site survey to create the physical and logical topology map.

In a wired network, the *physical topology* map consists of the wiring closet and the wiring to the individual end-user stations. In a wireless network, the physical topology consists of the wiring closet and an access point. Because there are no wires, the physical topology contains the wireless signal coverage area.

The *logical topology* is generally the same for a wired and wireless network. It includes the naming and Layer 3 addressing of end stations, router gateways, and other network devices, regardless of the physical location. It indicates the location of routing, network address translation, and firewall filtering.

Refer to
Figure
in online course

To develop a logical topology requires understanding the relationship between the devices and the network, regardless of the physical cabling layout. There are several topological arrangements possible. Examples include star, extended star, partial mesh, and full mesh topologies.

Star Topologies

With a star topology, each device is connected via a single connection to a central point. The central point is typically a switch or a wireless access point. The advantage of a star topology is that if a single connecting device fails, only that device is affected. However, if the central device, such as the switch, fails, then all connecting devices lose connectivity.

An extended star is created when the central device in one star is connected to a central device of another star, such as when multiple switches are interconnected, or daisy-chained together.

Mesh Topologies

Most Core Layers in a network are wired in either a full mesh or a partial mesh topology. In a full mesh topology, every device has a connection to every other device. While full mesh topologies provide the benefit of a fully redundant network, they can be difficult to wire and manage and are more costly.

For larger installations, a modified partial mesh topology is used. In a partial mesh topology, each device is connected to at least two other devices. This arrangement creates sufficient redundancy, without the complexity of a full mesh.

Implementing redundant links through partial or full mesh topologies ensures that network devices can find alternate paths to send data in the event of a failure.

3.1.3 Network Requirements Documentation

Refer to
Figure
in online course

Along with creating the topology maps for the existing network, it is necessary to obtain additional information about the hosts and networking devices that are currently installed. This information is recorded on a brief inventory sheet. The technician also documents any growth that the company anticipates in the near future.

This information helps the network designer determine what new equipment is required, and the best way to structure the network to support the anticipated growth.

The inventory sheet of the installed devices includes:

- Device name
- Date of purchase
- Warranty information
- Location
- Brand and model
- Operating system
- Logical addressing information
- Gateway
- Method of connectivity
- Virus Checker
- Security information

Refer to **Packet Tracer Activity** for this chapter

Packet Tracer Activity

Create a logical and physical network diagram.

View printable instructions.

3.2 Planning

3.2.1 Network Upgrade Planning Phases

Refer to
Figure
in online course

A network upgrade requires extensive planning. Just like any project, a need is identified and then a plan outlines the process from beginning to end. A good project plan helps identify any strengths, weaknesses, opportunities, or threats (*SWOT*). The plan clearly defines the tasks, and the order in which the tasks are to be completed.

Examples of good planning:

- Sports teams follow game plans

- Builders follow blueprints

- Ceremonies or meetings follow agendas

A network that is a patchwork of devices strung together, using a mixture of technologies and protocols, is usually an indicator of poor initial planning. These types of networks are susceptible to downtime, and are difficult to maintain and troubleshoot.

Planning a network upgrade begins after the site survey and the resulting report are completed. There are five distinct phases.

Refer to **Figure** in online course

Phase 1: Requirements Gathering

After all of the information has been gathered from the customer and the site visit, it is analyzed to determine the network requirements. This analysis is done by the design team at the ISP, which creates an Analysis Report.

Phase 2: Selection and Design

Devices and cabling are selected based on the requirements outlined in the *Analysis Report*. Multiple design options are created and regularly shared with other members on the project. This phase allows team members to view the network from a documentation perspective and evaluate trade-offs in performance and cost. It is during this step that any weaknesses of the design can be identified and addressed.

Also during this phase, prototypes are created and tested. A *prototype* is a good indicator of how the new network will operate.

When the design is approved by the customer, implementation of the new network can begin.

Phase 3: Implementation

If the first two steps are done correctly, the implementation phase is more likely to be performed without incident. If there are tasks that have been overlooked in the earlier phases, they must be corrected during implementation. Creating an implementation schedule that allows time for unexpected events, keeps disruption for the customer to a minimum. Staying in constant communication with the customer during the installation is critical to the success of the project.

Refer to **Figure** in online course

Phase 4: Operation

The network is brought into service in what is called a *production environment*. Prior to this step, the network is considered to be in a testing or implementation phase.

Phase 5: Review and Evaluation

After the network is in operation, the design and implementation must be reviewed and evaluated. For this process, the following steps are recommended:

Step 1: Compare the user experience with the goals in the documentation, and evaluate if the design is right for the job.

Step 2: Compare the projected designs and costs with the actual deployment. This evaluation ensures that future projects will benefit from the lessons learned on this project.

Step 3: Monitor the operation and record changes. It is important that the system is always fully documented and accountable.

Careful planning at each phase ensures that the project goes smoothly and that the installation is successful. On-site technicians are often included in the planning, because they participate in all phases of the upgrade.

Refer to **Interactive Graphic** in online course.

Activity

Determine if an action is part of the Requirements Gathering, Selection and Design, Implementation, Operation, or Review and Evaluation phase.

Based on the statement, select the appropriate phase.

3.2.2 Physical Environment

Refer to **Figure** in online course

One of the first things that the network designer does to select the equipment and design of the new network is to examine the existing network facilities and cabling. The facilities include the physical environment, the telecommunication room, and the existing network wiring. A *telecommunications room*, or wiring closet, in a small, single-floor network is usually referred to as the Main Distribution Facility (*MDF*).

The MDF typically contains many of the network devices, including switches or hubs, routers, and access points. It is where all of the network cable concentrates to a single point. Many times, the MDF also contains the Point of Presence (POP) of the ISP, where the network makes the connection to the Internet through a telecommunications service provider.

If additional wiring closets are required, they are referred to as Intermediate Distribution Facilities (IDFs). IDFs are typically smaller than the MDF, and connect to the MDF.

Many small businesses do not have a telecommunications room or closet. Network equipment may be located on a desk or other furniture, and wires could be just lying on the floor. Network equipment must always be secure. As a network grows, a telecommunications room is critical to the security and reliability of the network.

3.2.3 Cabling Considerations

Refer to **Figure** in online course

When the existing cabling is not up to specification for the new equipment, new cabling must be planned for and installed. The condition of the existing cabling can quickly be determined by the physical inspection of the network during the site visit. When planning the installation of network cabling, there are four physical areas to consider:

- User work areas

- Telecommunications room

- Backbone area

- Distribution area

There are many different types of cable found in the networking environment, and some are more common than others:

- *Shielded twisted pair (STP)* - Usually Category 5, 5e, or 6 cable that has a foil shielding to protect from outside electromagnetic interference (EMI). In an Ethernet environment, the distance limitation is approximately 328 feet (100 meters).

- *Unshielded twisted pair (UTP)* - Usually Category 5, 5e, or 6 cable that does not provide extra shielding from EMI, but it is inexpensive. Cable runs should avoid electrically noisy areas. In an Ethernet environment, the distance limitation is approximately 328 feet (100 meters).

- *Fiber-optic cable* - A medium that is not susceptible to EMI, and can transmit data faster and farther than copper. Depending on the type of fiber optics, distance limitations can be several miles (kilometers). Fiber-optic can be used for backbone cabling and high-speed connections.

In addition to these three commonly-used cabling types, coaxial is also used in networking. Coaxial is not typically used in LANs, but it is widely used in cable modem provider networks. Coaxial has a solid copper core with several protective layers including polyvinyl chloride (PVC), braided wire shielding, and a plastic covering. Distance is several miles (kilometers). Limitations depend on the purpose of the connection.

There are several organizations in the world that provide LAN cabling specifications.

Refer to
Figure
in online course

The Telecommunications Industry Association (TIA) and the Electronic Industries Alliance (EIA) worked together to provide the TIA/EIA cable specifications for LANs. Two of the most common TIA/EIA cable specifications include the 568-A and 568-B standards. Both of these standards typically use the same Cat 5 or Cat 6 cable, but with a different termination color code.

There are three different types of twisted pair cables that are used in networks:

- *Straight-through* - Connects dissimilar devices, such as a switch and a computer, or a switch and a router.

- *Crossover* - Connects similar devices, such as two switches or two computers.

- **Console** (or Rollover) - Connects a computer to the console port of a router or switch to do initial configuration.

Another cable type that is common in networks is a *serial cable*. A serial cable is typically used to connect the router to an Internet connection. This Internet connection may be to the phone company, the cable company, or a private ISP.

3.2.4 Structured Cable

Refer to
Figure
in online course

When designing a structured cable project, the first step is to obtain an accurate floor plan. The floor plan allows the technician to identify possible wiring closet locations, cable runs, and which electrical areas to avoid.

After the technician has identified and confirmed the locations of network devices, it is time to draw the network on the floor plan. Some of the more important items to document include the following:

- *Patch cable* - Short cable from the computer to the wall plate in the user work area

- *Horizontal cable* - Cable from the wall plate to the IDF in the distribution area

- *Vertical cable* - Cable from the IDF to the MDF in the backbone area of the business

- *Backbone cable* - Network part that handles the major traffic

- *Location of wiring closet* - Area to concentrate the end-user cables to the hub or switch

- *Cable management system* - Trays and straps used to guide and protect cable runs

- *Cable labeling system* - Labeling system or scheme to identify cables

■ *Electrical considerations* - Outlets and other items to support the electrical requirements of the network equipment

Refer to
Lab Activity
for this chapter

Lab Activity

Evaluate a floor plan and propose upgrades to accommodate extra floor space.

3.3 Purchasing and Maintaining Equipment

3.3.1 Purchasing Equipment

Refer to
Figure
in online course

As the ISP team plans the network upgrade, issues related to purchasing new equipment and the maintenance of new and existing equipment must be addressed. There are generally two options for obtaining new equipment:

■ *Managed service* - The equipment is obtained from the ISP through a lease or some other agreement, and the ISP is responsible for updating and maintaining the equipment.

■ *In-house* - The customer purchases the equipment, and the customer is responsible for the updates, warranties, and maintenance of the equipment.

When acquiring equipment, cost is always a major factor. A good cost analysis of the various options provides a sound basis for the final decision.

If a managed service is chosen, there are lease costs and possibly other service costs as outlined in the Service Level Agreement (SLA).

If the equipment is purchased outright, the customer should be aware of the price of the equipment, warranty coverage, compatibility with existing equipment, and update and maintenance issues. All of these must be analyzed to determine the cost-effectiveness of the purchase.

3.3.2 Selecting Network Devices

Refer to
Figure
in online course

After analyzing requirements, the design staff recommends the appropriate network devices to connect and support the new network functionality.

Modern networks use a variety of devices for connectivity. Each device has certain capabilities to control the flow of data across a network. A general rule is that the higher the device is in the OSI model, the more intelligent it is. What this means is that a higher level device can better analyze the data traffic and forward it based on information not available at lower layers. As an example, a Layer 1 hub can forward data only out of all ports, while a Layer 2 switch can filter the data and send it only out of the port that is connected to the destination based on the MAC address.

As switches and routers evolve, the distinction between them may seem blurred. One simple distinction remains: LAN switches provide connectivity within the local-area networks of the organization, while routers interconnect local networks and are needed in a wide-area network environment.

In addition to switches and routers, there are other connectivity options available for LANs. Wireless access points allow computers and other devices, such as handheld IP phones, to wirelessly connect to the network or share broadband connectivity. Firewalls guard against network threats and provide security and network control and containment.

Integrated Service Routers (ISRs) are network devices that combine the functionality of switches, routers, access points, and firewalls into the same device.

3.3.3 Selecting LAN Devices

Refer to
Figure
in online course

Although both a hub and a switch can provide connectivity at the Access Layer of a network, switches should be chosen for connecting devices to a LAN. Switches are more expensive than hubs, but the enhanced performance makes switches more cost-effective. A hub is generally chosen as a networking device only within a very small LAN, a LAN that requires little *throughput* requirements, or when finances are limited.

When selecting a switch for a particular LAN, there are a number of factors to consider. These factors include, but are not limited to:

- Speed and the types of ports and interfaces involved

- Expandability

- Manageability

- Cost

Speed and Types of Ports and Interfaces

Choosing Layer 2 devices that can accommodate increased speeds allows the network to evolve without replacing the central devices.

When selecting a switch, choosing the appropriate number and type of ports is critical.

Network designers should consider carefully how many twisted pair (TP) and fiber-optic ports are needed. It is also important to estimate how many more ports will be required to support network expansion.

Refer to
Figure
in online course

Expandability

Networking devices come in both fixed and modular physical configurations. Fixed configurations have a specific type and number of ports or interfaces. Modular devices have expansion slots that provide the flexibility to add new modules as requirements evolve. Most modular devices come with a minimum number of fixed ports and expansion slots.

A typical use of an expansion slot is to add fiber-optic modules to a device originally configured with a number of fixed TP ports. Modular switches can be a cost-effective approach to scaling LANs.

Manageability

A basic, inexpensive switch is not configurable. A managed switch that uses a Cisco IOS feature set allows control over individual ports or over the switch as a whole. Controls include the ability to change the settings for a device, add port security, and monitor performance.

For example, with a managed switch, ports can be turned on or off. In addition, administrators can control which computers or devices are allowed to connect to a port.

Refer to
Figure
in online course

Cost

The cost of a switch is determined by its capacity and features. The switch capacity includes the number and types of ports available and the overall throughput. Other factors that affect the cost are network management capabilities, embedded security technologies, and advanced switching technologies.

Using a simple cost-per-port calculation, it may initially appear that the best option is to deploy one large switch at a central location. However, this apparent cost savings may be offset by the expense of the longer cable lengths required to connect every device on the LAN to one switch. This option should be compared with the cost of deploying a number of smaller switches connected by a few long cables to a central switch.

Deploying a number of smaller devices, instead of a single large device, also has the benefit of reducing the size of the *failure domain*. A failure domain is the area of the network affected when a piece of networking equipment malfunctions or fails.

After the LAN switches are selected, determine which router is appropriate for the customer.

Refer to **Packet Tracer Activity** for this chapter

Packet Tracer Activity

Explore different LAN switch options.

Refer to **Figure** in online course

3.3.4 Selecting Internetworking Devices

A router is a Layer 3 device. It performs all tasks of devices in lower layers and selects the best route to the destination based on Layer 3 information. Routers are the primary devices used to interconnect networks. Each port on a router connects to a different network and routes packets between the networks. Routers have the ability to break up broadcast domains and collision domains.

When selecting a router, it is necessary to match the characteristics of the router to the requirements of the network. Factors for choosing a router include:

- Type of connectivity required
- Features available
- Cost

Connectivity

Routers interconnect networks that use different technologies. They can have both LAN and WAN interfaces.

The LAN interfaces of the router connect to the LAN media. The media is typically UTP cabling, but modules can be added for using fiber optics. Depending on the series or model of router, there can be multiple interface types for connecting LAN and WAN cabling.

Refer to **Figure** in online course

Features

It is necessary to match the characteristics of the router to the requirements of the network. After analysis, the business management may determine that it needs a router with specific features. In addition to basic routing, features include:

- Security
- Quality of Service (QoS)
- Voice over IP (VoIP)
- Network Address Translation (*NAT*)
- Dynamic Host Configuration Protocol (DHCP)
- Virtual Private Network (*VPN*)

Cost

Budget is an important consideration when selecting internetwork devices. Routers can be expensive, and additional modules, such as fiber optic modules, can increase the cost.

An Integrated Service Router (ISR) is a relatively new technology that combines multiple services into one device. Before the introduction of the ISR, multiple devices were required to meet the needs of data, wired, wireless, voice, video, firewall, and VPN technologies. The ISR was designed with multiple services to accommodate the demands of small- to medium-sized businesses and branch offices of large organizations. With an ISR, an organization can quickly and easily enable end-to-end protection for users, applications, network endpoints, and wireless LANs. In addition, the cost of an ISR can be less than if the individual devices were purchased separately.

Refer to **Packet Tracer Activity** for this chapter

Packet Tracer Activity

Explore different internetworking device options.

3.3.5 Network Equipment Upgrades

Refer to **Figure** in online course

Many small networks were initially built using a low-end integrated router to connect wireless and wired users. These routers are designed to support small networks, usually consisting of a few wired hosts and possibly four or five wireless devices. When a small business outgrows the capabilities of their existing network devices, it is necessary to upgrade to more robust devices. Within this course, examples of these devices are the Cisco 1841 ISR and the Cisco 2960 Switch.

The Cisco 1841 is designed to be a branch office or medium-sized business router. As an entry-level multiservice router, it offers a number of different connectivity options. It is modular in design and can deliver multiple security services.

Refer to **Figure** in online course

Some of the features of the Catalyst 2960 switches are:

- Entry-level, enterprise-class, fixed-configuration switching that is optimized for Access Layer deployments

- Fast Ethernet and Gigabit Ethernet to desktop configurations

- Ideal for entry-level enterprise, mid-market, and branch-office environments

- Compact size for deployments outside of the wiring closet

These switches can provide the high speeds and high-density switching capabilities that the smaller ISRs with integrated switching cannot. They are a good option when upgrading networks built with either hubs or small ISR devices.

The Cisco Catalyst 2960 Series Intelligent Ethernet Switches are a family of fixed-configuration, standalone devices that provide Fast Ethernet and Gigabit Ethernet connectivity to the desktop.

3.3.6 Design Considerations

Refer to **Figure** in online course

Purchasing network devices and installing cables are only the beginning of the network upgrade process. Networks must also be reliable and available. Reliability can be achieved by adding redundant components to the network, such as two routers instead of one. In this instance, alternate data paths are created, so if one router is experiencing problems, the data can take an alternate route to arrive at the destination.

An increase in reliability leads to improved availability. For example, telephone systems require five-9s of availability. This means that the telephone system must be available 99.999% of the time. Telephone systems cannot be down, or unavailable, for more than .001% of the time.

Fault tolerance systems are typically used to improve network reliability. Fault tolerance systems include devices such as a UPS, multiple AC power supplies, hot-swappable devices, multiple interface cards, and backup systems. When one device fails, the redundant or backup system takes over to ensure minimal loss of reliability. Fault tolerance can also include backup communication links.

Refer to
Figure
in online course

IP Addressing Plan

Planning for a network installation must include planning the logical addressing. Changing the Layer 3 IP addressing is a major issue when upgrading a network. If the structure of the network is going to be changed in the upgrade, the IP address scheme and network information may need to be altered.

The plan should include every device that requires an IP address, and account for future growth. The hosts and network devices that require an IP address include:

- User computers

- Administrator computers

- Servers

- Other end devices such as printers, IP phones, and IP cameras

- Router LAN interfaces

- Router WAN (serial) interfaces

There are other devices that may need an IP address to access and manage them. These include:

- Standalone switches

- Wireless Access Points

For example, if a new router is introduced to the network, each interface on that router can be used to create additional networks, or subnets. These new subnets need to have the proper IP address and subnet mask calculated. Sometimes, this means having to assign a totally new addressing scheme to the network.

After all of the planning and design phases are complete, the upgrade proceeds to the implementation phase, in which the actual network installation begins.

Chapter Summary

Click through the buttons for summary information.

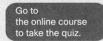

Chapter Quiz

Take the chapter quiz to check your knowledge.

Your Chapter Notes

CHAPTER 4

Planning the Addressing Structure

Introduction

Refer to
Figure
in online course

4.1 IP Addressing in the LAN

Refer to
Figure
in online course

4.1.1 Review of IP Addresses

One of the most important aspects of communications on an internetwork is the IP addressing scheme.

IP addressing is the method used to identify hosts and network devices. As the Internet grew over time and the number of hosts connected to it increased, IP addressing schemes had to adapt to cope with the growth.

While IP addressing schemes have had to adapt, the basic IP address structure for IPv4 remains the same. To send and receive messages on an IP network, every network host must be assigned a unique 32-bit IP address. Because large binary numbers are difficult for people to read and understand, IP addresses are usually displayed in ***dotted-decimal notation***. In dotted-decimal notation, each of the four octets is converted to a decimal number separated by a decimal point. For example, the IP address:

11000000.10101000.00000001.01101010

is represented as 192.168.1.106 in dotted-decimal notation.

Refer to
Figure
in online course

IP addresses are hierarchical. A hierarchy is like a family tree with parents at the top and children connected to them below. For a network, this means that part of the 32-bit number identifies the network (parent), while the rest of the bits identify the host (child). In the early days of the Internet, there were so few organizations needing to connect to the Internet, that networks were assigned by only the first 8 bits (first ***octet***) of the IP address. This left the remaining 24 bits to be used for local host addresses.

The 8-bit network designation made sense at first, because originally people thought that the Internet would be made up of a few very large universities, governments, and military organizations. Using only 8 bits for the network number enabled the creation of 256 separate networks, each containing over 16 million hosts. It soon became apparent that more organizations, and eventually individuals, were connecting to the Internet to do research and to communicate with others. More networks were required, and a way to assign more network numbers had to be created.

Refer to
Figure
in online course

To create more possible network designations, the 32-bit address space was organized into five classes. Three of these classes, A, B, and C, provide addresses that can be assigned to individual hosts or networks. The other two classes, D and E, are reserved for *multicast* and experimental use.

Until this change, routers examined only the first 8-bits of an IP address for the network ID. Class B networks, however, use the first 16 bits to identify the network. Class C networks use the first 24 bits to identify the network. With this addition, routers needed to be programmed to look beyond the first 8 bits to identify class B and C networks.

It was decided to divide the networks in a manner that would make it easy for routers and hosts to determine the correct number of *network ID* bits. The class of a network is indicated by the values of the first few bits of the IP address, called the *high-order bit*s. If the first bit is 0, the network is a Class A, and the first octet represents the network ID. When the first bit is 1, the router examines the second bit. If that bit is 0, the network is a Class B, and the router uses the first 16 bits for the network ID. If the first three bits are 110, it indicates a Class C address. Class C addresses use the first 24 bits, or three octets, to designate the network. Dividing the original 8-bit network into smaller network classes increased the number of available network designations from 256 to over two million.

Refer to
Figure
in online course

In addition to creating separate classes, the Internet Engineering Task Force (*IETF*) decided to reserve some of the Internet address space for use by private networks. Private networks have no connection to public networks. *Private network address*es are not to be routed across the Internet. This allows multiple networks in various locations to use the same private addressing scheme without creating addressing conflicts.

The use of private address space reduced the number of unique registered IP addresses that were assigned to organizations.

A single Class A address, 10.0.0.0, was reserved for private use. In addition, address space in classes B and C was also set aside for private networks.

Most networks today use a private address structure. Most consumer networking devices, by default, give out private addresses through DHCP. Only the devices that connect directly to the Internet are assigned registered Internet routable addresses.

4.1.2 Subnetting a Network

Refer to
Figure
in online course

Networks continued to grow and connect to the Internet throughout the 1980s and into the 1990s, with many organizations adding hundreds, and even thousands, of hosts to their network. An organization with thousands of hosts should have been well served by a Class B network, however, there were some problems.

First, organizations with thousands of hosts rarely had them all in one place. Some organizations wanted to separate individual departments from each other for security or management purposes. Second, a primary type of packet forwarded on a network is the broadcast packet. Broadcast packets are forwarded to all hosts within a single logical network. With thousands of hosts on a single network sending broadcast traffic, and limited bandwidth available, network performance significantly decreased as more hosts were added.

To solve these problems, the organizations leading the development of the Internet chose to partition their networks into mini-networks, or subnetworks, using a process called subnetting. How can a single IP network get split into multiple networks so that each subnet is treated as a separate network?

RFC 917, Internet Subnets, defines the subnet mask as the method routers use to isolate the network portion from an IP address. When a router receives a packet, it uses the destination IP address in the packet and the subnet masks associated with the routes in its routing table to determine the appropriate path on which to forward the packet.

The router reads the subnet mask from left to right, bit by bit. If a bit in the subnet mask is set to 1, it indicates that the value in that position is part of the network ID. A 0 in the subnet mask indicates that the value in that position is part of the host ID.

Refer to
Figure
in online course

In the original IP address hierarchy, there are two levels: a network and a host. In a classful addressing scheme, the first three leading bit values are used to determine that an IP address is either a Class A, B, or C. When an address is identified by class, the number of bits that make up the network ID and the number of bits that make up the *host ID* are known. The default subnet masks for the network classes are:

Class A 255.0.0.0

Class B 255.255.0.0

Class C 255.255.255.0

Subdividing a classful network adds a level to the network hierarchy. Now there are three levels: a network, a subnetwork, and a host. How can the subnet mask be modified to indicate the new hierarchical level?

A single Class A, B, or C network address space can be divided into multiple subnetworks by using bits from the host address space to designate the subnet ID. As an example, an organization using a Class C address space has two offices in different buildings. To make the network easier to manage, the network administrators want each location to have a logically separate network. Taking two bits from the host address increases the subnet mask length from the default 24 bits to 26 bits, or 255.255.255.192.

When bits are borrowed from the host portion of the address to identify the subnet, fewer bits are available for individual hosts. If two bits are used for the subnet ID, only six bits are left in the host portion of the address.

Refer to
Figure
in online course

With traditional *classful subnet*ting, the same number of host bits is used to designate the subnet ID for all the resulting *subnet*works. This type of subnetting always results in a fixed number of subnets and a fixed number of hosts per subnet. For this reason, this is known as fixed-length subnetting.

The decision about how many host bits to use for the subnet ID is a big planning decision. There are two considerations when planning subnets: the number of hosts on each network, and the number of individual local networks needed. The table for the subnet possibilities for the 192.168.1.0 network shows how the selection of a number of bits for the subnet ID affects both the number of possible subnets and the number of hosts that can be in each subnet.

One thing to keep in mind is that in all IPv4 networks, two host addresses are reserved: the all-0s and the all-1s. An address with all 0s in the host portion of the address is an invalid host address and usually refers to the entire network or subnetwork. An address with all 1s in the host portion is used as the local network broadcast address. When a network is subnetted, each subnet contains an all-0s and an all-1s host address that cannot be used for individual host addresses.

4.1.3 Custom Subnet Masks

Refer to
Figure
in online course

When a network is partitioned, the router must use a modified or custom subnet mask to distinguish the subnets from each other.

A default subnet mask and a custom subnet mask differ from each other in that the default subnet masks only change on octet boundaries. For instance, the default subnet mask for a Class A network is 255.0.0.0. Custom subnet masks take bits from the host ID portion of the IP address and add them to the default subnet mask.

To create a *custom subnet mask*, the first question to answer is how many bits to take from the host ID to add to the subnet mask? The number of bits to borrow to meet a specific number of subnets can be determined by the math equation: 2^n, where n equals the number of bits borrowed.

If three subnets are required, there must be enough subnet bits to allow for three unique subnet addresses.

For example, if starting with a Class C address, such as 192.168.1.0, there are only eight host bits to borrow from. Each bit can only be a 1 or a 0. To allow for three subnets, at least two of the eight bits must be borrowed. This creates four subnets total:

00 - 1st subnet

01 - 2nd subnet

10 - 3rd subnet

11 - 4th subnet

In the above example, two bits were borrowed, $2^2 = 4$ or 2 x 2 = 4, so four subnets were created. If between five and eight subnets were needed, then three bits would be required ($2^3 = 8$ or 2 x 2 x 2).

The number of bits selected for the subnet ID affects both the number of possible subnets and the number of hosts that can be in each subnet.

Refer to
Figure
in online course

With classed subnetting, the number of bits required for the subnet ID depends on two factors: the number of subnets created and the number of hosts per subnet.

In classed, or fixed-length, subnetting, all subnets must be the same size, which means that the maximum number of hosts that each subnet can support is the same for all subnets created. The more bits that are taken for the subnet ID, the fewer bits left for host IDs.

The same base equation, 2^n, with a slight modification, can be used to determine the number of host IDs available based on the number of host bits remaining. Because each subnet has two host addresses that are reserved, the all-0s and all-1s addresses, the equation to determine the number of hosts supported is modified to $2^n - 2$.

After it is determined how many bits make up the subnet address, all devices on the network are informed of the subdivision by the subnet mask. With the subnet mask, it is possible to tell which subnet an IP address is in and to design simple classful subnetted IP address schemes.

Refer to
Figure
in online course

Subnetting solved a number of problems that existed with the original classed network address spaces. It permitted organizations that owned a class A, B, or C address to subdivide their address space into smaller local subnets to more efficiently assign addresses. However, subnetting is also important in helping to minimize traffic loads and for adding security measures between networks.

An example of a situation that might require subnetting is an ISP customer that has outgrown its initial network installation. In this network, the original small, integrated wireless router is overloaded with traffic from both wired and wireless users. Because of its relatively small size, a Class C address space is used to address the network.

One possible solution to the problem of the overloaded network is to add a second networking device, such as a larger integrated service router (ISR). When adding a device, it is a good practice to place the wired and wireless users on separate local subnetworks to increase security. The original wireless router can still be used to provide the wireless users with connectivity and security on one network. Hubs or switches connecting the wired users can then be directly connected to the new

ISR using a different network. The ISR and the wireless router can then be directly connected with a third network.

This new network configuration requires that the existing Class C network be divided into at least three subnetworks. Using classful subnetting, at least two bits must be taken from the host portion of the address to meet the customer requirements. This subnetting scheme results in the creation of four individual networks, each with 62 available host addresses (64 possible addresses, minus the all-0s and all-1s addresses).

Refer to **Interactive Graphic** in online course.

Activity

Given the network address and the subnet mask, define the range of hosts, the broadcast address, and the next network address.

Click the octet in the table to enter your answer.

Refer to **Packet Tracer Activity** for this chapter

Packet Tracer Activity

Subnet a network to meet the requirements of multiple LANs.

4.1.4 VLSM and Classless Inter-Domain Routing (CIDR)

Refer to **Figure** in online course

The original classful subnetting design required that all subnets of a single classed network be the same size. This was because routers did not include subnet mask information in their routing updates. A router programmed with one subnet address and mask on an interface automatically applied that same mask to the other network subnets in its routing table. This limitation required planning for fixed-length subnet masks in the IP addressing scheme.

However, fixed-length subnet masks can waste a significant number of IP addresses. For example, an organization with one site has approximately 8,000 hosts and three other locations with 1,000, 400, and 100 hosts, respectively. With a fixed-length subnet mask, each subnet would have to support at least 8,000 hosts, even the one assigned to the location needing only 100 addresses.

Variable length subnet masking (VLSM) helps to solve this issue. VLSM addressing allows an address space to be divided into networks of various sizes. This is done by subnetting subnets. To accomplish this, routers today must receive routing information that includes the IP address of the network, and the subnet mask information which indicates the number of bits that make up the network portion of the IP address. VLSM saves thousands of IP addresses that would be wasted with traditional classful subnetting.

In addition to VLSM, Classless Inter-Domain Routing (*CIDR*) was proposed in RFC 1519 and accepted. CIDR ignores network classes based on the value of the high-order bits. CIDR identifies networks based solely on the number of bits in the network prefix, which corresponds to the number of 1s in the subnet mask. An example of an IP address written using CIDR notation is 172.16.1.1/16, where the /16 represents the number of bits in the network prefix.

Refer to **Figure** in online course

CIDR protocols freed routers from using only the high-order bits to determine the network prefix. Removing that restriction eliminated the need to allocate registered IP addresses by address class.

Before CIDR, an ISP requiring 3,000 host addresses could request either a full Class B address space or multiple Class C network addresses to meet its requirements. With a Class B address space, the ISP would waste thousands of registered addresses. If it requested multiple Class C addresses, it could be difficult to design the ISP network so that no single section required more than 254 host addresses. Routing tables containing many Class C addresses can also get large and difficult to manage.

By ignoring the traditional address classes, CIDR enables the ISP to request a block of addresses based on the number of host addresses it requires. Supernets, created by combining a group of Class C addresses into one large block, enable addresses to be assigned more efficiently. An example of a supernet is 192.168.0.0/19. Using the first 19 bits of the IP address for the network prefix enables this supernet to contain 8,190 possible host addresses. An ISP can use a supernet as one large network or divide it into as many smaller networks as needed to meet its requirements.

In this example of a supernet, the private Class C address of 192.168.0.0 is used. In reality, most networks that use private addressing use either the Class A or B reserved addresses and subnetting. Although classed addressing and fixed-length subnet masking are becoming less common, it is important to understand how these addressing methods work. Many devices still use the default subnet mask if no custom subnet mask is specified.

4.1.5 Communicating Between Subnets

Refer to
Figure
in online course

When a network is split into subnets, each subnet is actually a completely separate network. Therefore, for a device in one subnet to communicate with a device in another subnet, a router is required because routers connect networks.

To determine how many hosts are needed in each subnet, it is necessary to include the router interface, or gateway interface, and the individual host devices. Each router interface must have an IP address in the same subnet as the host network attached to it.

In some instances, it may be necessary to connect two routers, such as when connecting the Linksys device and the 1841 ISR. This configuration must ensure that interfaces on routers that connect to each other are assigned IP addresses in the same network or subnet. Here the common link shows the two routers connected on the 192.168.1.16/29 subnet with host IP addresses of 192.168.1.17/29 and 192.168.1.18/29.

Refer to **Packet Tracer Activity** for this chapter

Packet Tracer Activity

Modify the addresses, subnet masks, and device default gateways to enable routing between subnets.

Refer to
Lab Activity
for this chapter

Lab Activity

Create an IP addressing scheme for a small network.

4.2 NAT and PAT

4.2.1 Basic Network Address Translation (NAT)

Refer to
Figure
in online course

Routers are required to route between subnets on an internal network, regardless of whether the IP address range is public or private. However, if the address range is private, private networks cannot be routed across the public Internet. Therefore, how do host devices using a private addressing scheme communicate across the Internet? Network Address Translation (NAT) must be enabled on the device connecting the private network to the ISP network.

NAT allows a large group of private users to access the Internet by sharing one or more public IP addresses. Address translation is similar to how a telephone system works in a company. As a company adds employees, at some point, they no longer run a public phone line directly to each employee desk. Instead, they use a system that allows the company to assign each employee an extension number. The company can do this because not all employees use the phone at the same time. Using private extension numbers enables the company to purchase a smaller number of external phone lines from the phone company.

NAT works similarly to a company phone system. Saving registered IP addresses is one of the main reasons that NAT was developed. NAT can also provide security to PCs, servers, and networking devices by withholding their actual IP host addresses from direct Internet access.

Refer to
Figure
in online course

The main advantages of NAT are that IP addresses can be re-used and many hosts on a single LAN can share globally unique IP addresses. NAT operates transparently and helps shield users of a private network against access from the public domain.

In addition, NAT hides private IP addresses from public networks. The advantage to this is that NAT operates much like an access control list, not allowing outside users to access internal devices. The disadvantage is that additional configurations are required to allow access from legitimate, external users.

Another disadvantage is that NAT has an impact on some applications that have IP addresses in their *message payload*, because these IP addresses must also be translated. This translation increases load on the router and hinders network performance.

4.2.2 IP NAT Terms

Refer to
Figure
in online course

When configuring NAT on a router, there are a few terms that help explain how the router accomplishes NAT:

- *Inside local network* - Refers to any network connected to a router interface that is part of the privately addressed LAN. Hosts on inside networks have their IP addresses translated before they are transmitted to outside destinations.

- *Outside global network* - Any network attached to the router that is external to the LAN and does not recognize the private addresses assigned to hosts on the LAN.

- *Inside local address* - Private IP address configured on a host on an inside network. The address must be translated before it can travel outside the local network addressing structure.

- *Inside global address* - IP address of an inside host as it appears to the outside network. This is the translated IP address.

- *Outside local address* - Destination address of the packet while it is on the local network. Usually, this address is the same as the outside global address.

- *Outside global address* - Public IP address of an external host. The address is allocated from a globally routable address or network space.

Refer to
Interactive Graphic
in online course.

Activity

Match the NAT terminology to the source and destination of the *datagram*.

Drag and drop the Inside and Outside options to the correct address type.

4.2.3 Static and Dynamic NAT

Refer to
Figure
in online course

Addresses can be assigned dynamically. Dynamic NAT allows hosts on a private network that have private IP addresses to access a public network, such as the Internet. Dynamic NAT occurs when a router assigns an outside global address from a pre-defined address, or pool of addresses, to an inside private network device.

As long as the session is open, the router watches for the inside global address and sends acknowledgments to the initiating inside device. When the session ends, the router simply returns the inside global address to the pool.

Refer to
Figure
in online course

One of the advantages of using NAT is that individual hosts are not directly accessible from the public Internet. But what if one or more of the hosts within a network are running services that need to be accessed from Internet connected devices and devices on the local private LAN?

One way to provide access to a local host from the Internet is to assign that device a static address translation. Static translations ensure that an individual host private IP address is always translated to the same registered global IP address. It ensures that no other local host is translated to the same registered address.

Static NAT allows hosts on the public network to access selected hosts on a private network. If a device on the inside network needs to be accessible from the outside, use *static NAT*.

Both static and dynamic NAT can be configured at the same time, if necessary.

Refer to **Packet Tracer Activity** for this chapter

Packet Tracer Activity

Examine the contents of the IP header as traffic crosses the NAT border.

4.2.4 Port-based Network Address Translation (PAT)

Refer to
Figure
in online course

When an organization has a very small registered *IP address pool*, or perhaps even just a single IP address, it can still enable multiple users to simultaneously access the public network with a mechanism called NAT overload, or Port Address Translation (*PAT*). PAT translates multiple local addresses to a single global IP address.

When a source host sends a message to a destination host, it uses an IP address and port number combination to keep track of each individual conversation with the destination host. In PAT, the gateway translates the local source address and port combination in the packet to a single global IP address and a unique port number above 1024. Although each host is translated into the same global IP address, the port number associated with the conversation is unique.

Responding traffic is addressed to the translated IP address and port number used by the host. A table in the router contains a list of the internal IP address and port number combinations that are translated to the external address. Responding traffic is directed to the appropriate internal address and port number. Because there are over 64,000 ports available, a router is unlikely to run out of addresses, which could happen with dynamic NAT.

Refer to
Figure
in online course

Because each translation is specific to the local address and local port, each connection, which generates a new source port, requires a separate translation. For example, 10.1.1.1:1025 requires a separate translation from 10.1.1.1:1026.

The translation is only in place for the duration of the connection, so a given user does not keep the same global IP address and port number combination after the conversation ends.

Users on the outside network cannot reliably initiate a connection to a host on a network that uses PAT. Not only is it impossible to predict the local or global port number of the host, but a gateway does not even create a translation unless a host on the inside network initiates the communication.

Refer to
Lab Activity
for this chapter

Lab Activity

Determine the number of Port Address Translations being performed.

4.2.5 IP NAT Issues

Refer to
Figure
in online course

People access the Internet from private networks without ever realizing that the router is using NAT. However, an important issue with NAT is the additional workload necessary to support IP address and port translations.

Some applications increase the workload of the router, because they embed an IP address as part of the encapsulated data. The router must replace the source IP addresses and port combinations that are contained within the data, and the source addresses in the IP header.

With all this activity taking place within a router, NAT implementation requires good network design, careful selection of equipment and accurate configuration.

NAT has become so commonplace in integrated networking devices used in homes and small businesses, that for some people, configuring it is a matter of selecting a check box. As businesses grow and require more sophisticated gateway and routing solutions, device configurations for NAT become more complex.

Refer to
Figure
in online course

Subnetting networks, private IP addressing, and the use of NAT were developed to provide a temporary solution to the problem of IP address depletion. These methods, though useful, do not create more IP addresses. As a response to address depletion, *IPv6* was proposed in 1998 with RFC 2460.

Although its primary purpose was to solve IPv4 IP address depletion, there were other good reasons for its development. Since IPv4 was first standardized, the Internet has grown significantly. This growth has uncovered advantages and disadvantages of IPv4, and the possibility for upgrades to include new capabilities.

A general list of improvements that IPv6 proposes are:

- More address space

- Better address space management

- Easier TCP/IP administration

- Modernized routing capabilities

- Improved support for multicasting, security, and mobility

The development of IPv6 is designed to address as many of these requests and problems as possible.

Refer to
Figure
in online course

With IPv6, IP addresses are 128 bits with a potential address space of 2^{128}. In decimal notation, that is approximately a 3 followed by 38 zeroes. If IPv4 address space was represented by a small marble, then IPv6 address space is represented by a volume almost equivalent to the planet Saturn.

Working with 128-bit numbers is difficult, so the IPv6 address notation represents the 128 bits as 32 hexadecimal digits, which are further subdivided into eight groups of four hexadecimal digits, using colons as delimiters. The IPv6 address has a three-part hierarchy. The global prefix is the first three blocks of the address and is assigned to an organization by an Internet names registry. The subnet and the interface ID are controlled by the network administrator.

Network administrators will have some time to adjust to this new IPv6 structure. Before the widespread adoption of IPv6 occurs, network administrators still need a way to more efficiently use private address spaces.

Chapter Summary

Click through the buttons for summary information.

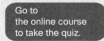

Chapter Quiz

Take the chapter quiz to check your knowledge.

Your Chapter Notes

CHAPTER 5

Configuring Network Devices

Introduction

Refer to
Figure
in online course

5.1 Initial ISR Router Configuration

5.1.1 ISR

Refer to
Figure
in online course

The Cisco Integrated Services Router (ISR) is one of the most popular networking devices to meet the growing communications needs of businesses. The ISR combines features such as routing and LAN switching functions, security, voice, and WAN connectivity into a single device. This makes the ISR ideal for small to medium-sized businesses and for ISP-managed customers.

The optional integrated switch module allows small businesses to connect LAN devices directly to the 1841 ISR. With the integrated switch module, if the number of LAN hosts exceeds the number of switch ports, additional switches or hubs can be connected in a daisy chain to extend the number of LAN ports available. If the switch module is not included, external switches are connected to the router interfaces of the ISR.

The ISR routing function allows a network to be broken into multiple local networks using subnetting and supports internal LAN devices connecting to the Internet or WAN.

Refer to
Figure
in online course

The Cisco Internetwork Operating System (IOS) software provides features that enable a Cisco device to send and receive network traffic using a wired or wireless network. Cisco IOS software is offered to customers in modules called images. These images support various features for businesses of every size.

The entry-level Cisco IOS software image is called the IP Base image. The Cisco IOS IP Base software supports small to medium-sized businesses and supports routing between networks.

Other Cisco IOS software images add services to the IP Base image. For example, the Advanced Security image provides advanced security features, such as private networking and firewalls.

Many different types and versions of Cisco IOS images are available. Images are designed to operate on specific models of routers, switches, and ISRs.

It is important to know which image and version is loaded on a device before beginning the configuration process.

5.1.2 Physical Setup of the ISR

Refer to
Figure
in online course

Each ISR is shipped with the cables and documentation needed to power up the device and begin the installation. When a new device is received, it is necessary to unpack the device and verify that all the hardware and equipment is included.

Items shipped with a new Cisco 1841 ISR include:

- RJ-45 to DB-9 console cable

- DB-9 to DB-25 modem adapter

- Power cord

- Product registration card, called the Cisco.com card

- Regulatory compliance and safety information for Cisco 1841 routers

- Router and Security Device Manager (SDM) Quick Start guide

- Cisco 1800 Series Integrated Services Router (Modular) Quick Start guide

Refer to
Figure
in online course

To install a new Cisco 1841 ISR requires special tools and equipment, which most ISPs and technician labs usually have available. Any additional equipment required depends on the model of the device and any optional equipment ordered.

Typically, the tools required to install a new device include:

- PC with a terminal emulation program, such as HyperTerminal

- Cable ties and a No. 2 Phillips screwdriver

- Cables for WAN interfaces, LAN interfaces, and USB interfaces

It may also be necessary to have equipment and devices required for WAN and broadband communication services, such as a modem. Additionally, Ethernet switches may be required to connect LAN devices or expand LAN connectivity, depending on whether the integrated switch module is included and the number of LAN ports required.

Refer to
Figure
in online course

Before beginning any equipment installation, be sure to read the Quick Start guide and other documentation that is included with the device. The documentation contains important safety and procedural information to prevent accidental damage to the equipment during installation.

Follow these steps to power up an 1841 ISR.

1. Securely mount and ground the device chassis, or case.

2. Seat the external compact flash card.

3. Connect the power cable.

4. Configure the terminal emulation software on the PC and connect the PC to the console port.

5. Turn on the router.

6. Observe the startup messages on the PC as the router boots up.

5.1.3 Bootup Process

Refer to
Figure
in online course

The router bootup process has three stages.

1. Perform Power-on self test (POST) and load the bootstrap program.

The POST is a process that occurs on almost every computer when it boots up. POST is used to test the router hardware. After POST, the bootstrap program is loaded.

2. Locate and load the Cisco IOS software.

The bootstrap program locates the Cisco IOS software and loads it into RAM. Cisco IOS files can be located in one of three places: flash memory, a *TFTP* server, or another location indicated in the startup configuration file. By default, the Cisco IOS software loads from flash memory. The configuration settings must be changed to load from one of the other locations.

3. Locate and execute the startup configuration file or enter setup mode.

After the Cisco IOS software is loaded, the bootstrap program searches for the startup configuration file in NVRAM. This file contains the previously saved configuration commands and parameters, including interface addresses, routing information, passwords, and other configuration parameters.

If a configuration file is not found, the router prompts the user to enter setup mode to begin the configuration process.

If a startup configuration file is found, it is copied into RAM and a prompt containing the host name is displayed. The prompt indicates that the router has successfully loaded the Cisco IOS software and configuration file.

Refer to
Figure
in online course

To avoid the loss of data, it is important to have a clear understanding of the difference between the startup configuration file and the running configuration file.

Startup Configuration File

The startup configuration file is the saved configuration file that sets the properties of the device each time the device is powered up. This file is stored in non-volatile RAM (NVRAM), meaning that it is saved even when power to the device is turned off.

When a Cisco router is first powered up, it loads the Cisco IOS software to working memory, or RAM. Next, the startup configuration file is copied from NVRAM to RAM. When the startup configuration file is loaded into RAM, the file becomes the initial running configuration.

Running Configuration File

The term running configuration refers to the current configuration running in RAM on the device. This file contains the commands used to determine how the device operates on the network.

The running configuration file is stored in the working memory of the device. Changes to the configuration and various device parameters can be made when the file is in working memory. However, the running configuration is lost each time the device is shut down, unless the running configuration is saved to the startup configuration file.

Changes to the running configuration are not automatically saved to the startup configuration file. It is necessary to manually copy the running configuration to the startup configuration file.

When configuring a device via the Cisco command line interface (CLI) the command `copy running-config startup-config`, or the abbreviated version `copy run start`, saves the running configuration to the startup configuration file. When configuring a device via the Cisco SDM GUI, there is an option to save the router running configuration to the startup configuration file each time a command is completed.

Refer to
Figure
in online course

After the startup configuration file is loaded and the router boots successfully, the `show version` command can be used to verify and troubleshoot some of the basic hardware and software components used during the bootup process. The output from the `show version` command includes:

■ The Cisco IOS software version being used.

- The version of the system bootstrap software, stored in ROM memory, that was initially used to boot the router.

- The complete filename of the Cisco IOS image and where the bootstrap program located it.

- Type of CPU on the router and amount of RAM. It may be necessary to upgrade the amount of RAM when upgrading the Cisco IOS software.

- The number and type of physical interfaces on the router.

- The amount of NVRAM. NVRAM is used to store the startup-config file.

- The amount of flash memory on the router. Flash is used to permanently store the Cisco IOS image. It may be necessary to upgrade the amount of flash when upgrading the Cisco IOS software.

- The current configured value of the software configuration register in hexadecimal.

The configuration register tells the router how to boot up. For example, the factory default setting for the configuration register is 0x2102. This value indicates that the router attempts to load a Cisco IOS software image from flash and loads the startup configuration file from NVRAM. It is possible to change the configuration register and, therefore, change where the router looks for the Cisco IOS image and the startup configuration file during the bootup process. If there is a second value in parentheses, it denotes the configuration register value to be used during the next reload of the router.

Refer to
Figure
in online course

There are times when the router does not successfully boot. This failure can be caused by a number of factors, including a corrupt or missing Cisco IOS file, an incorrect location for the Cisco IOS image specified by the configuration register, or inadequate memory to load a new Cisco IOS image. If the router fails to boot the IOS, it then boots up in ROM monitor (ROMmon) mode. ROMmon software is a simple command set stored in read only memory (ROM) that can be used to troubleshoot boot errors and recover the router when the IOS is not present.

When the router boots up to ROMmon mode, one of the first steps in troubleshooting is to look in flash memory for a valid image using the `dir flash:` command. If an image is located, attempt to boot the image with the `boot flash:` command.

rommon 1>**boot flash:c2600-is-mz.121-5**

If the router boots properly with this command, there are two possible reasons why the Cisco IOS image did not load from flash initially. First, use the `show version` command to check the configuration register to ensure that it is configured for the default boot sequence. If the configuration register value is correct, use the `show startup-config` command to see if there is a `boot system` command that instructs the router to use a different location for the Cisco IOS image.

Refer to
Lab Activity
for this chapter

Lab Activity

Power up an ISR and view the router system and configuration files using show commands.

5.1.4 Cisco IOS Programs

Refer to
Figure
in online course

There are two methods to connect a PC to a network device to perform configuration and monitoring tasks: out-of-band management and in-band management.

Out-of-band Management

Out-of-band management requires a computer to be directly connected to the console port or auxiliary port (AUX) of the network device being configured. This type of connection does not require the local network connections on the device to be active. Technicians use out-of-band management to initially configure a network device, because until properly configured, the device cannot participate in the network. Out-of-band management is also useful when the network connectivity is not functioning correctly and the device cannot be reached over the network. Performing out-of-band management tasks requires a terminal emulation client installed on the PC.

In-band Management

Use in-band management to monitor and make configuration changes to a network device over a network connection. For a computer to connect to the device and perform in-band management tasks, at least one network interface on the device must be connected to the network and be operational. Either Telnet, *HTTP* or SSH can be used to access a Cisco device for in-band management. A web browser or a Telnet client program can be used to monitor the network device or make configuration changes.

Refer to
Figure
in online course

The Cisco IOS command line interface (CLI) is a text-based program that enables entering and executing Cisco IOS commands to configure, monitor, and maintain Cisco devices. The Cisco CLI can be used with either in-band or out-of-band management tasks.

Use CLI commands to alter the configuration of the device and to display the current status of processes on the router. For experienced users, the CLI offers many time-saving features for creating both simple and complex configurations. Almost all Cisco networking devices use a similar CLI. When the router has completed the power-up sequence, and the `Router>` prompt appears, the CLI can be used to enter Cisco IOS commands.

Technicians familiar with the commands and operation of the CLI find it easy to monitor and configure a variety of different networking devices. The CLI has an extensive help system that assists users in setting up and monitoring devices.

Refer to
Figure
in online course

In addition to the Cisco IOS CLI, other tools are available to assist in configuring a Cisco router or ISR. Security Device Manager (SDM) is a web-based GUI device management tool. Unlike CLI, SDM can be used only for in-band management tasks.

SDM Express simplifies the initial router configuration. It uses a step-by-step approach to create a basic router configuration quickly and easily.

The full SDM package offers more advanced options, such as:

- Configuring additional LAN and WAN connections

- Creating firewalls

- Configuring VPN connections

- Performing security tasks

SDM supports a wide range of Cisco IOS software releases and is available free of charge on many Cisco routers. SDM is pre-installed on the flash memory of the Cisco 1800 Series ISR. If the router has SDM installed, it is good practice to use SDM to perform the initial router configuration. This configuration is done by connecting to the router via a preset network port on the router.

Refer to
Figure
in online course

Not all Cisco devices support SDM. In addition, SDM does not support all the commands that are available through the CLI. Consequently, it is sometimes necessary to use the CLI to complete a device configuration that is started using SDM. Familiarity with both methods is critical to successfully support Cisco devices.

Refer to
Interactive Graphic
in online course.

Activity

Determine when to use CLI or SDM.

Based on the description, check CLI or SDM.

5.2 Using Cisco SDM Express and SDM

5.2.1 Cisco SDM Express

Refer to
Figure
in online course

When adding a new device to a network, it is critical to ensure that the device functions correctly. The addition of one poorly configured device can cause an entire network to fail.

Configuring a networking device, such as a router, can be a complex task, no matter which tool is used to enter the configuration. Therefore, follow best practices for installing a new device to ensure that all device settings are properly configured and documented.

Refer to
Figure
in online course

Cisco SDM Express is a tool bundled within the Cisco Router and Security Device Manager that makes it easy to create a basic router configuration. To start using SDM Express, connect an Ethernet cable from the PC NIC to the Ethernet port specified in the quick start guide on the router or ISR being configured.

SDM Express uses eight configuration screens to assist in creating a basic router configuration:

- Overview
- Basic Configuration
- LAN IP Address
- DHCP
- Internet (WAN)
- Firewall
- Security Settings
- Summary

The SDM Express GUI provides step-by-step guidance to create the initial configuration of the router. After the initial configuration is completed, the router is available on the LAN. The router can also have a WAN connection, a firewall, and up to 30 security enhancements configured.

5.2.2 SDM Express Configuration Options

Refer to
Figure
in online course

The SDM Express Basic Configuration screen contains basic settings for the router that is being configured. The following information is required:

- *Host name -* The name assigned to the router being configured.
- *Domain name for the organization -* An example of a domain name is cisco.com, but domain names can end with a different suffix, such as .org or .net.
- *Username and password -* The username and password used to access SDM Express to configure and monitor the router. The password must be at least six characters long.
- *Enable secret password -* The password that controls user access to the router, which affects the ability to make configuration changes using the CLI, Telnet, or the console ports. The password must be at least six characters long.

Refer to
Figure
in online course

The LAN configuration settings enable the router interface to participate on the connected local network.

- *IP address -* Address for the LAN interface in dotted-decimal format. It can be a private IP address if the device is installed in a network that uses Network Address Translation (NAT) or Port Address Translation (PAT).

It is important to take note of this address. When the router is restarted, this address is the one used to access SDM Express, not the address that was provided in the Quick Start guide.

- *Subnet mask* - Identifies the network portion of the IP address.

- *Subnet bits* - Number of bits used to define the network portion of the IP address. The number of bits can be used instead of the subnet mask.

- *Wireless parameters* - Optional. Appear if the router has a wireless interface, and Yes was clicked in the Wireless Interface Configuration window. Specifies the SSID of the wireless network.

Refer to
Figure
in online course

DHCP is a simple way to assign IP addresses to host devices. DHCP dynamically allocates an IP address to a network host when the host is powered up, and reclaims the address when the host is powered down. In this way, addresses can be reused when hosts no longer need them. Using SDM Express, a router can be configured as a DHCP server to assign addresses to devices, such as PCs, on the internal local network.

To configure a device for DHCP, select the **Enable DHCP Server on the LAN Interface** check-box. Checking this box enables the router to assign private IP addresses to devices on the LAN. IP addresses are leased to hosts for a period of one day.

DHCP uses a range of allowable IP addresses. By default, the valid address range is based on the IP address and subnet mask entered for the LAN interface.

The starting address is the lowest address in the IP address range. The starting IP address can be changed, but it must be in the same network or subnet as the LAN interface.

The ending IP address is the highest address in the IP address range and it can be changed to decrease the pool size. It must be in the same network as the IP starting address.

Refer to
Figure
in online course

Additional DHCP configuration parameters include:

- *Domain name for the organization* - This name is given to the hosts as part of the DHCP configuration.

- *Primary domain name server* - IP address of the primary DNS server. Used to resolve URLs and names on the network.

- *Secondary domain name server* - IP address of a secondary DNS sever, if available. Used if the primary DNS server does not respond.

Selecting **Use these DNS values for DHCP clients** enables the DHCP server to assign DHCP clients with the configured DNS settings. This option is available if a DHCP server has been enabled on the LAN interface.

Refer to
Interactive Graphic
in online course.

Activity

Identify the configuration parameters from the SDM Express.

Drag the Configuration Parameter to the information that must be entered.

5.2.3 Configuring WAN Connections Using SDM Express

Refer to
Figure
in online course

Configuring an Internet (WAN) Connection

A serial connection can be used to connect networks that are separated by large geographic distances. These WAN network interconnections require a telecommunications service provider (TSP).

Serial connections are usually lower speed links, compared to Ethernet links, and require additional configuration. Prior to setting up the connection, determine the type of connection and protocol *encapsulation* required.

The protocol encapsulation must be the same at both ends of a serial connection. Some encapsulation types require authentication parameters, like username and password, to be configured. Encapsulation types include:

- High-Level Data Link Control (HDLC)
- Frame Relay
- Point-to-Point Protocol (PPP)

Refer to
Figure
in online course

The WAN configuration window has additional WAN parameters.

Address Type List

Depending on the type of encapsulation selected, different methods of obtaining an IP address for the serial interface are available:

- *Static IP address* - Available with Frame Relay, PPP, and HDLC encapsulation types. To configure a static IP address, enter the IP address and subnet mask.
- *IP unnumbered* - Sets the serial interface address to match the IP address of one of the other functional interfaces of the router. Available with Frame Relay, PPP, and HDLC encapsulation types.
- *IP negotiated* - The router obtains an IP address automatically through PPP.
- *Easy IP (IP Negotiated)* - The router obtains an IP address automatically through PPP.

Refer to
Lab Activity
for this chapter

Lab Activity

Configure an ISR using Cisco SDM Express

5.2.4 Configuring NAT Using Cisco SDM

Refer to
Figure
in online course

Either Cisco SDM Express or Cisco SDM can be used to configure a router.

SDM supports many of the same features that SDM Express supports; however, SDM has more advanced configuration options. For this reason, after the router basic configuration is completed using SDM Express, many users switch to SDM. For example, enabling NAT requires the use of SDM.

The Basic NAT Wizard configures Dynamic NAT with PAT, by default. PAT enables the hosts on the internal local network to share the single registered IP address assigned to the WAN interface. In this manner, hosts with internal private addresses can have access to the Internet.

Only the hosts with the internal address ranges specified in the SDM configuration are translated. It is important to verify that all address ranges that need access to the Internet are included.

Steps for configuring NAT include:

Step 1. Enable NAT configuration using SDM.

Step 2. Navigate through the Basic NAT Wizard.

Step 3. Select the interface and set IP ranges.

Step 4. Review the configuration.

Refer to
Lab Activity
for this chapter

Lab Activity

Configure Dynamic NAT using the Cisco SDM basic NAT wizard.

5.3 Configuring a Router Using IOS CLI

5.3.1 Command Line Interface Modes

Refer to
Figure
in online course

Using the Cisco IOS CLI to configure and monitor a device is very different from using SDM. The CLI does not provide step-by-step configuration assistance; therefore, it requires more planning and expertise to use.

CLI Command Modes

The Cisco IOS supports two levels of access to the CLI: user EXEC mode and privileged EXEC mode.

When a router or other Cisco IOS device is powered up, the access level defaults to user EXEC mode. This mode is indicated by the command line prompt:

Router>

Commands that can be executed in user EXEC mode are limited to obtaining information about how the device is operating, and troubleshooting using some **show** commands and the ping and traceroute utilities.

To enter commands that can alter the operation of the device requires privileged level access. Enable the privileged EXEC mode by entering **enable** at the command prompt and pressing Enter.

The command line prompt changes to reflect the mode change. The prompt for privileged EXEC mode is:

Router#

To disable the privileged mode and return to user mode, enter **disable** at the command prompt.

Both modes can be protected with a password, or a username and password combination.

Refer to
Figure
in online course

Various configuration modes are used to set up a device. Configuring a Cisco IOS device begins with entering privileged EXEC mode. From privileged EXEC mode, the user can access the other configuration modes.

In most cases, commands are applied to the running configuration file using a terminal connection. To use these commands, the user must enter global configuration mode.

To enter global configuration, type the command **configure terminal** or **config t.** Global configuration mode is indicated by the command line prompt:

Router(config)#

Any commands entered in this mode take effect immediately and can alter the operation of the device.

From global configuration mode, the administrator can enter other sub-modes.

Interface configuration mode is used to configure LAN and WAN interfaces. To access interface configuration mode, from global configuration type the command **interface** [*type*] [*number*]. Interface configuration mode is indicated by the command prompt:

Router(config-if)#

Another commonly used sub-mode is the router configuration submode represented by the following prompt:

Router(config-router)#

This mode is used to configure routing parameters.

Refer to
Lab Activity
for this chapter

E-Lab Activity

Using the Cisco CLI explore the various configuration modes.

5.3.2 Using the Cisco IOS CLI

Refer to
Figure
in online course

The Cisco IOS CLI is full of features that help in recalling commands needed to configure a device. These features are one reason why network technicians prefer to use the Cisco IOS CLI to configure routers.

The context-sensitive help feature is especially useful when configuring a device. Entering **help** or the **?** at the command prompt displays a brief description of the help system.

Router# **help**

Context-sensitive help can provide suggestions for completing a command. If the first few characters of a command are known but the exact command is not, enter as much of the command as possible, followed by a **?**. Note that there is no space between the command characters and the **?**.

Additionally, to get a list of the parameter options for a specific command, enter part of the command, followed by a space, and then the **?**. For example, entering the command **configure** followed by a space and a **?** shows a list of the possible variations. Choose one of the entries to complete the command string. Once the command string is completed, a <cr> appears. Press Enter to issue the command.

If a **?** is entered and nothing matches, the help list will be empty. This indicates that the command string is not a supported command.

Refer to
Figure
in online course

Users sometimes make a mistake when typing a command. The CLI indicates if an unrecognized or incomplete command is entered. The % symbol marks the beginning of an error message. For example, if the command **interface** is entered with no other parameters, an error message displays indicating an incomplete command:

% Incomplete command

Use the **?** to get a list of the available parameters.

If an incorrect command is entered, the error message would read:

% Invalid input detected

It is sometimes hard to see the mistake within an incorrectly entered command. Fortunately, the CLI provides an error indicator. The caret symbol (^) appears at the point in the command string where there is an incorrect or unrecognized character. The user can return to the point where the error was made and use the help function to determine the correct command to use.

Refer to
Figure
in online course

Another feature of the Cisco IOS CLI is the ability to recall previously typed commands. This feature is particularly useful for recalling long or complex commands or entries.

The command history is enabled by default and the system records 10 command lines in the history buffer. To change the number of command lines the system records during a session, use the **terminal history size** or the **history size** command. The maximum number of command lines is 256.

To recall the most recent command in the history buffer, press **Ctrl-P** or the **Up Arrow** key. Repeat this process to recall successively older commands. To return to a more recent command in the history buffer, press **Ctrl-N** or the **Down Arrow** key. Repeat this process to recall successively more recent commands.

The CLI recognizes partially typed commands based on their first unique character. For example, type **int** instead of **interface**. If a short cut, such as **int** is entered, pressing the Tab key will automatically complete the entire command entry of **interface**.

On most computers, additional select and copy functions are available using various function keys. A previous command string may be copied and then pasted or inserted as the current command entry.

Refer to
Interactive Graphic
in online course.

Activity

Match the commands to their function.

Drag the correct keystroke combination to the proper definition.

Refer to **Packet Tracer Activity** for this chapter

Packet Tracer Activity

Explore the features of the Cisco IOS CLI.

5.3.3 Using Show Commands

Refer to
Figure
in online course

The Cisco IOS CLI includes show commands that display relevant information about the configuration and operation of the device.

Network technicians use the show commands extensively for viewing configuration files, checking the status of device interfaces and processes, and verifying the device operational status. Show commands are available whether the device was configured using the CLI or SDM.

The status of nearly every process or function of the router can be displayed using a show command. Some of the more popular show commands are:

- `show running-config`
- `show interfaces`
- `show arp`
- `show ip route`
- `show protocols`
- `show version`

Refer to
Lab Activity
for this chapter

E-Lab Activity

Use the show run and show interface commands to answer questions about the router configuration.

Refer to **Packet Tracer Activity** for this chapter

Packet Tracer Activity

Use Cisco IOS show commands on a router located at the ISP.

5.3.4 Basic Configuration

Refer to
Figure
in online course

The initial configuration of a Cisco IOS device involves configuring the device name and then the passwords that are used to control access to the various functions of the device.

A device should be given a unique name as one of the first configuration tasks. This task is accomplished in global configuration mode with the following command.

```
Router(config)# hostname [name]
```

When the Enter key is pressed, the prompt changes from the default host name, which is Router, to the newly configured host name.

The next configuration step is to configure passwords to prevent access to the device by unauthorized individuals.

The **enable password** and **enable secret** commands are used to restrict access to privileged EXEC mode, preventing unauthorized users from making configuration changes to the router.

```
Router(config)# enable password [password]
Router(config)# enable secret [password]
```

The difference between the two commands is that the enable password is not encrypted by default. If the enable password is set, followed by the enable secret password, the **enable secret** command overrides the **enable password** command.

Refer to
Figure
in online course

Other basic configurations of a router include configuring a banner, enabling synchronous logging, and disabling domain lookup.

Banners

A banner is text that a user sees when initially logging on to the router. Configuring an appropriate banner is part of a good security plan. At a very minimum, a banner should warn against unauthorized access. Never configure a banner that welcomes an unauthorized user.

There are two types of banners: message-of-the-day (MOTD) and login information. The purpose for two separate banners is to be able to change one without affecting the entire banner message.

To configure the banners, the commands are **banner motd** and **banner login**. For both types, a delimiting character, such as a #, is used at the beginning and at the end of the message. The delimiter allows the user to configure a multiline banner.

If both banners are configured, the login banner appears after the MOTD but before the login credentials.

Synchronous Logging

The Cisco IOS software often sends unsolicited messages, such as a change in the state of a configured interface. Sometimes these messages occur in the middle of typing a command. The message does not affect the command, but can cause the user confusion when typing. To keep the unsolicited output separate from the typed input, the **logging synchronous** command can be entered in global configuration mode.

Disabling Domain Lookup

By default, when a host name is entered in enable mode, the router assumes that the user is attempting to telnet to a device. The router tries to resolve unknown names entered in enable mode by sending them to the DNS server. This process includes any words entered that the router does not recognize, including mistyped commands. If this capability is not wanted, the **no ip domain-lookup** command turns off this default feature.

Refer to
Figure
in online course

There are multiple ways to access a device to perform configuration tasks. One of these ways is to use a PC attached to the console port on the device. This type of connection is frequently used for initial device configuration.

Setting a password for console connection access is done in global configuration mode. These commands prevent unauthorized users from accessing user mode from the console port.

```
Route(config)# line console 0
 Router(config)# password [password]
Router(config)# login
```

When the device is connected to the network, it can be accessed over the network connection. When the device is accessed through the network, it is considered a vty connection. The password must be configured on the vty port.

```
Route(config)# line vty 0 4
  Router(config)# password [password]
Router(config)# login
```

0 4 represents 5 simultaneous in-band connections. It is possible to set a different password for each connection by specifing specific line connection numbers, such as **line vty 0**.

To verify that the passwords are set correctly, use the `show running-config` command. These passwords are stored in the running-configuration in clear text. It is possible to set encryption on all passwords stored within the router so that they are not easily read by unauthorized individuals. The global configuration command `service password-encryption` ensures that all passwords are encrypted.

Remember, if the running configuration is changed, it must be copied to the startup configuration file or the changes are lost when the device is powered down. To copy the changes made to the running configuration back to the stored startup configuration file, use the `copy run start` command.

Packet Tracer Activity

Use Cisco IOS CLI to perform an initial router configuration.

5.3.5 Configuring An Interface

To direct traffic from one network to another, router interfaces are configured to participate in each of the networks. A router interface connecting to a network will typically have an IP address and subnet mask assigned that is within the host range for the connected network.

There are different types of interfaces on a router. Serial and Ethernet interfaces are the most common. Local network connections use Ethernet interfaces.

WAN connections require a serial connection through an ISP. Unlike Ethernet interfaces, serial interfaces require a clock signal to control the timing of the communications, called a clock rate. In most environments, data communications equipment (DCE) devices, such as a modem or CSU/DSU, provide the clock rate.

When a router connects to the ISP network using a serial connection, a CSU/DSU is required if the WAN is digital. A modem is required if the WAN is analog. These devices convert the data from the router into a form acceptable for crossing the WAN, and convert data from the WAN into an acceptable format for the router. By default, Cisco routers are data terminal equipment (DTE) devices. Because the DCE devices control the timing of the communication with the router, the Cisco DTE devices accept the clock rate from the DCE device.

Though uncommon, it is possible to connect two routers directly together using a serial connection. In this instance, no CSU/DSU or modem is used, and one of the routers must be configured as a DCE device to provide clocking. If the router is connected as the DCE device, a clock rate must be set on the router interface to control the timing of the DCE/DTE connection.

Configuring an interface on the router must be done in global configuration mode. Configuring an Ethernet interface is very similar to configuring a serial interface. One of the main differences is that a serial interface must have a clock rate set if it is acting as a DCE device.

The steps to configure an interface include:

Step 1. Specify the type of interface and the interface port number.

Step 2. Specify a description of the interface.

Step 3. Configure the interface IP address and subnet mask.

Step 4. Set the clock rate, if configuring a serial interface as a DCE.

Step 5. Enable the interface.

After an interface is enabled, it may be necessary to turn off an interface for maintenance or troubleshooting. In this case, use the `shutdown` command.

When configuring the serial interface on a 1841, the serial interface is designated by 3 digits, C/S/P, where C=Controller#, S=Slot# and P=Port#. The 1841 has two modular slots. The designation Serial0/0/0 indicates that the serial interface module is on controller 0, in slot 0, and that the interface to be used is the first one (0). The second interface is Serial0/0/1. The serial module is normally installed in slot 0 but may be installed in slot 1. If this is the case, the designation for the first serial interface would be Serial0/1/0 and the second would be Serial0/1/1.

For built in ports, such as the FastEthernet ports the designation is 2 digits, C/P, where C=Controller#, and P=Port#. The designation Fa0/0 represents controller 0 and interface 0.

Refer to
Lab Activity
for this chapter

E-Lab Activity

Configure the serial interfaces on two routers.

Refer to **Packet Tracer Activity**
for this chapter

Packet Tracer Activity

Configure the Ethernet and Serial interfaces of a router.

Refer to
Lab Activity
for this chapter

Lab Activity

Configure basic settings on a router using the Cisco IOS CLI.

5.3.6 Configuring a Default Route

Refer to
Figure
in online course

A router forwards packets from one network to another based on the destination IP address specified in the packet. It examines the routing table to determine where to forward the packet to reach the destination network. If the router does not have a route to a specific network in its routing table, a default route can be configured to tell the router how to forward the packet. The default route is used by the router only if the router does not know where to send a packet.

Usually, the default route points to the next hop router on the path to the Internet. The information needed to configure the default route is the IP address of the next hop router, or the interface that the router uses to forward traffic with an unknown destination network.

Configuring the default route on a Cisco ISR must be done in global configuration mode.
```
Router(config)# ip route 0.0.0.0 0.0.0.0 [next-hop-IP-address]
```
or

Refer to **Packet Tracer Activity**
for this chapter

```
Router(config)# ip route 0.0.0.0 0.0.0.0 [interface-type] [number]
```
Packet Tracer Activity

Configure a default route on routers in a medium-sized business network topology.

5.3.7 Configuring DHCP Services

Refer to
Figure
in online course

The Cisco IOS CLI can be used to configure a router to function as a DHCP server.

Using a router configured with DHCP simplifies the management of IP addresses on a network. The administrator needs to update only a single, central router when IP configuration parameters change. Configuring DHCP using the CLI is a little more complex than configuring it using SDM.

There are eight basic steps to configuring DHCP using the CLI.

Step 1. Create a DHCP address pool.

Step 2. Specify the network or subnet.

Step 3. Exclude specific IP addresses.

Step 4. Specify the domain name.

Step 5. Specify the IP address of the DNS server.

Step 6. Set the default gateway.

Step 7. Set the lease duration.

Step 8. Verify the configuration.

Refer to **Packet Tracer Activity** for this chapter

Packet Tracer Activity

Configure a router as a DHCP server for attached clients.

Refer to **Lab Activity** for this chapter

Lab Activity

Use the Cisco SDM and IOS CLI to configure a router as a DHCP server.

5.3.8 Configuring Static NAT Using Cisco IOS CLI

Refer to **Figure** in online course

NAT enables hosts with internal private addresses to communicate on the Internet. When configuring NAT, at least one interface must be configured as the inside interface. The inside interface is connected to the internal, private network. Another interface, usually the external interface used to access the Internet, must be configured as the outside interface. When devices on the internal network communicate out through the external interface, the addresses are translated to one or more registered IP addresses.

There are occasions when a server located on an internal network must be accessible from the Internet. This accessibility requires that the server has a specific registered address that external users can specify. One way to provide this address to an internal server is to configure a static translation.

Static NAT ensures that addresses assigned to hosts on the internal network are always translated to the same registered IP address.

Configuring NAT and static NAT using the Cisco IOS CLI requires a number of steps.

Step 1. Specify the inside interface.

Step 2. Set the primary IP address of the inside interface.

Step 3. Identify the inside interface using the `ip nat inside` command.

Step 4. Specify the outside interface.

Step 5. Set the primary IP address of the outside interface.

Step 6. Identify the outside interface using the `ip nat outside` command.

Step 7. Define the static address translation.

Step 8. Verify the configuration.

Refer to **Figure** in online course

There are several router CLI commands to view NAT operations for verification and troubleshooting.

One of the most useful commands is `show ip nat translations`. The output displays the detailed NAT assignments. The command shows all static translations that have been configured and any dynamic translations that have been created by traffic. Each translation is identified by protocol and its inside and outside local and global addresses.

The `show ip nat statistics` command displays information about the total number of active translations, NAT configuration parameters, how many addresses are in the pool, and how many have been allocated.

Additionally, use the `show run` command to view NAT configurations.

By default, if dynamic NAT is configured, translation entries time out after 24 hours. It is sometimes useful to clear the dynamic entries sooner than 24 hours. This is especially true when testing the NAT configuration. To clear dynamic entries before the timeout has expired, use the `clear ip nat translation *` command in the enable mode. Only the dynamic translations are removed from the table. Static translations cannot be cleared from the translation table.

Packet Tracer Activity

Configure static NAT on a router.

Lab Activity

Configure PAT using Cisco SDM and static NAT using Cisco IOS CLI.

5.3.9 Backing Up a Cisco Router Configuration

After a router is configured, the running configuration should be saved to the startup configuration file. It is also a good idea to save the configuration file in another location, such as a network server. If the NVRAM fails or becomes corrupt and the router cannot load the startup configuration file, another copy is available. There are multiple ways that a configuration file can be saved.

One way configuration files can be saved to a network server is using TFTP. The TFTP server must be accessible to the router via a network connection.

Step 1. Enter the `copy startup-config tftp` command.

Step 2. Enter the IP address of the host where the configuration file will be stored.

Step 3. Enter the name to assign to the configuration file or accept the default.

Step 4. Confirm each choice by answering yes.

The running configuration can also be stored on a TFTP server using the `copy running-config tftp` command.

To restore the backup configuration file, the router must have at least one interface configured and be able to access the TFTP server over the network.

Step 1. Enter the `copy tftp running-config` command.

Step 2. Enter the IP address of the remote host where the TFTP server is located.

Step 3. Enter the name of the configuration file or accept the default name.

Step 4. Confirm the configuration filename and the TFTP server address.

Step 5. Using the `copy run start` command, copy the running-configuration to the startup-configuration file to ensure that the restored configuration is saved.

When restoring your configuration, it is possible to copy the tftp file to the startup configuration file. However, this does require a router reboot in order to load the startup configuration file into the running configuration.

Refer to
Figure
in online course

Another way to create a backup copy of the configuration is to capture the output of the **show running-config** command. To do this from the terminal session, copy the output, paste it into a text file, and then save the text file.

The following steps are used to capture the configuration from a HyperTerminal screen.

Step 1. Select **Transfer**.

Step 2. Select **Capture Text.**

Step 3. Specify a name for the text file to capture the configuration.

Step 4. Select **Start** to start capturing text.

Step 5. Use the **show running-config** command to display the configuration on the screen.

Step 6. Press the spacebar when each "-More -" prompt appears.

After the complete configuration has been displayed, the following steps stop the capture.

Step 1. Select **Transfer**.

Step 2. Select **Capture Text.**

Step 3. Select **Stop**.

After the capture is complete, the configuration file must be edited to remove extra text, such as the "building configuration" Cisco IOS message. Also, the **no shutdown** command must be added to the end of each interface section. Click **File > Save** to save the configuration. The configuration file can be edited from a text editor such as Notepad.

The backup configuration can be restored from a HyperTerminal session. Before the configuration is restored, any other configurations should be removed from the router using the **erase startup-config** command at the privileged EXEC prompt. The router is then restarted using the **reload** command.

The following steps copy the backup configuration to the router.

Step 1. Enter router global configuration mode.

Step 2. Select **Transfer > Send Text File** in HyperTerminal.

Step 3. Select the name of the file for the saved backup configuration.

Step 4. Restore the startup configuration with the **copy run start** command

Refer to **Packet Tracer Activity** for this chapter

Packet Tracer Activity

Back up the running configuration to a TFTP server.

Refer to **Lab Activity** for this chapter

Lab Activity

Use HyperTerminal to save and load the running configuration.

Refer to **Lab Activity** for this chapter

Lab Activity

Use TFTP to save and load the running configuration.

5.4 Connecting the CPE to the ISP

5.4.1 Installing the CPE

Refer to
Figure
in online course

One of the main responsibilities of an on-site network technician is to install and upgrade equipment located at a customer home or business. Network devices installed at the customer location are called customer premises equipment (*CPE*) and include devices such as routers, modems, and switches.

The installation or upgrade of a router can be disruptive for a business. Many businesses rely on the Internet for their correspondence and have e-commerce services that must be accessed during the day. Planning the installation or upgrade is a critical step in ensuring successful operation. Additionally, planning enables options to be explored on paper, where it is easy and inexpensive to correct errors.

The ISP technical staff usually meets with business customers for planning. During planning sessions, the technician determines the configuration of the router to meet customer needs and the network software that may be affected by the new installation or upgrade.

The technician works with the IT personnel of the customer to decide which router configuration to use and to develop the procedure that verifies the router configuration. From this information, the technician completes a configuration checklist.

The configuration checklist provides a list of the most commonly configured components. It typically includes an explanation of each component and the configuration setting. The list is a tool for ensuring that everything is configured correctly on new router installations. It is also helpful for troubleshooting previously configured routers.

There are many different formats for configuration checklists, including some that are quite complex. ISPs should ensure that support technicians have, and know how to use, router configuration checklists.

Refer to
Figure
in online course

When new equipment is required, the devices are typically configured and tested at the ISP site before being installed at the customer site. Anything that is not functioning as expected can be replaced or fixed immediately. If a router is being installed, the network technician makes sure that the router is fully configured and that the router configuration is verified.

When the router is known to be configured correctly, all network cables, power cables, management cables, manufacturer documentation, manufacturer software, configuration documentation, and the special tools needed for router installation are assembled. An inventory checklist is used to verify that all necessary equipment needed to install the router is present. Usually, the network technician signs the checklist, indicating that everything has been verified. The signed and dated inventory checklist is included with the router when it is packaged for shipping to the customer premises.

The router is now ready to be installed by the on-site technician. It is important to find a time that provides the minimum amount of disruption. It may not be possible to install or upgrade network equipment during normal business hours. If the installation will cause the network to be down, the network technician, the ISP sales person, and a representative of the company prepare a router installation plan. This plan ensures that the customer experiences a minimum of disruption in service while the new equipment is installed. Additionally, the router installation plan identifies who the customer contact is and what the arrangements are for access to the site after business hours. As part of the installation plan, an installation checklist is created to ensure that equipment is installed appropriately.

Refer to
Figure
in online course

The on-site network technician must install the router at the customer premises using the router installation plan and checklist. When installing customer equipment, it is important to complete the job in a professional manner. This means that all network cables are labeled and fastened together or run through proper cable management equipment. Excess lengths of cable are coiled and secured out of the way.

Documentation should be updated to include the current configuration of the router, and network diagrams should be updated to show the location of the equipment and cables installed.

After the router is successfully installed and tested, the network technician completes the installation checklist. The completed checklist is then verified by the customer representative. The verification of the router installation often involves demonstrating that the router is correctly configured and that services that depend on the router work as expected.

When the customer representative is satisfied that the router has been correctly installed and is operational, the customer signs and dates the checklist. Sometimes there is a formal acceptance document in addition to the checklist. This procedure is often called the sign-off phase. It is critical that the customer representative signs off on the job, because the ISP can then bill the customer for the work.

Installation Documentation

Refer to
Figure
in online course

When customer equipment is configured and installed on the customer premises, it is important to document the entire process. Documentation includes all aspects of equipment configuration, diagrams of equipment installation, and checklists to validate the correct installation. If a new configuration is needed, the documentation is compared with the previous router configuration to determine if and how the new configuration has changed. Activity logs are used to track modifications and access to equipment. Properly maintained activity logs help when troubleshooting problems.

The technician starts documenting the work during router installation. All cables and equipment are correctly labeled and indicated on a diagram to simplify future identification.

The technician uses the installation and verification checklist when installing a router. This checklist displays the tasks to be completed at the customer premises. The checklist helps the network technician avoid errors and ensures that the installation is done efficiently and correctly.

A copy of the final documentation is left with the customer.

5.4.2 Customer Connections over a WAN

Refer to
Figure
in online course

New equipment at the customer site must be connected back to the ISP to provide Internet services. When customer equipment is upgraded, it is sometimes necessary to also upgrade the type of connectivity provided by the ISP.

Wide Area Networks

When a company or organization has locations that are separated by large geographical distances, it may be necessary to use the telecommunications service provider (TSP) to interconnect the LANs at the different locations. The networks that connect LANs in geographically separated locations are referred to as wide area networks (WANs).

TSPs operate large regional networks that can span long distances. Traditionally, TSPs transported voice and data communications on separate networks. Increasingly, these providers are offering converged information network services to their subscribers.

Individual organizations usually lease connections through the TSP network. Although the organization maintains all the policies and administration of the LANs at both ends of the connection, the policies within the communications service provider network are controlled by the ISP.

ISPs sell various types of WAN connections to their clients. WAN connections vary in the type of connector used, in bandwidth, and in cost. As small businesses grow, they require the increased bandwidth offered by some of the more expensive WAN connections. One of the jobs at an ISP or medium-sized business is to assess what type of WAN connection is needed.

Refer to
Figure
in online course

There are three types of serial WAN connections.

Point-to-Point

A point-to-point connection is a predefined communications path from the customer premises through a TSP network. It is a dedicated circuit with fixed bandwidth available at all time. Point-to-point lines are usually leased from the TSP. These lines are often called leased lines. Point-to-point connections are typically the most expensive of the WAN connection types, and are priced based on the bandwidth required and the distance between the two connected points. An example of a point-to-point WAN connection is a T1 or E1 link.

Circuit-Switched

A circuit-switched connection functions similarly to the way a phone call is made over a telephone network. When making a phone call to a friend, the caller picks up the phone, opens the circuit, and dials the number. The caller hangs up the phone when finished and the closes the circuit. An example of a circuit-switched WAN connection is an *ISDN* or dialup connection.

Packet-Switched

In a packet-switched connection, networks have connections into the TSP switched network. Many customers share this TSP network. Instead of the circuit being physically reserved from source to destination, as in a circuit-switched network, each customer has its own virtual circuit. A virtual circuit is a logical path between the sender and receiver, not a physical path. An example of a packet-switched network is Frame Relay.

5.4.3 Choosing a WAN Connection

Refer to
Figure
in online course

When choosing a WAN, the decision is largely dependent on the bandwidth and cost of the WAN connection. Smaller businesses are not able to afford some of the more expensive WAN connection options, such as SONET or ATM WAN connections. They usually install the less expensive DSL, cable, and T1 connections. In addition, higher bandwidth WAN connections may not be available in geographically isolated locations. If the offices supported are close to an urban center, there are more WAN choices.

Another factor that affects the decision on which WAN to choose is how the business plans to use the connection. If the business provides services over the Internet, it may require higher upstream bandwidth. For example, if a business hosts a web server for an e-commerce business, it needs enough upstream bandwidth to accommodate the number of external customers that visit its site. On the other hand, if the business uses an ISP to manage its e-commerce site, the business does not need as much upstream bandwidth.

For some businesses, the ability to get a service level agreement (SLA) with their WAN connection affects their decision. Less expensive WAN connections like dialup, DSL, and cable typically do not come with an SLA, whereas more expensive connections do.

Refer to
Figure
in online course

There are many things to consider when planning a WAN upgrade. The ISP initiates the process by analyzing the customer needs and reviewing the available options. A proposal is then generated for the customer. The proposal addresses the existing infrastructure, the customer requirements, and possible WAN options.

Existing Infrastructure

This is an explanation of the current infrastructure being used by the business. It helps the customer understand how the existing WAN connection provides services to their home or business.

Customer Requirements

This section of the proposal describes why a WAN upgrade is necessary for the customer. It outlines where the current WAN connection does not meet the customer needs. It also includes a list of requirements that the new WAN connection must meet to satisfy the current and future customer requirements.

WAN Options

This is a list of all the available WAN choices with the corresponding bandwidth, cost, and other features that are applicable for the business is included in the proposal. The recommended choice is indicated, including possible other options.

The WAN upgrade proposal is presented to the business decision-makers. They review the document and consider the options. When they have made their decision, the ISP works with the customer to develop a schedule and coordinate the WAN upgrade process.

Refer to **Lab Activity** for this chapter

Lab Activity

Complete a WAN upgrade plan based on the business scenario presented.

5.4.4 Configuring WAN Connections

Refer to **Figure** in online course

How a WAN is configured depends on the type of WAN connection required. Some WAN connections support Ethernet interfaces. Other WAN connections support serial interfaces.

Leased-line WAN connections typically use a serial connection, and require a channel service unit and data service unit (CSU/DSU) to attach to the ISP network. The ISP equipment needs to be configured so that it can communicate through the CSU/DSU to the customer premises.

For a serial connection, it is important to have a preconfigured clock rate that is the same on both ends of the connection. The clock rate is set by the DCE device, which is typically the CSU/DSU. The DTE device, typically the router, accepts the clock rate set by the DCE.

The Cisco default serial encapsulation is HDLC. It can be changed to PPP, which provides a more flexible encapsulation and supports authentication by the remote device.

Refer to **Packet Tracer Activity** for this chapter

Packet Tracer Activity

Configure a serial WAN connection from a Cisco ISR to a CSU/DSU at an ISP.

5.5 Initial Cisco 2960 Switch Configuration

5.5.1 Standalone Switches

Refer to **Figure** in online course

Although the integrated swith module of the 1841 ISR is adequate for connecting a small number of hosts to the LAN, it may be necessary to add larger, more capable switches to support additional users as the network grows.

A switch is a device that directs a stream of messages from one port to another based on the destination MAC address within the frame. A switch cannot route traffic between two different local networks. In the context of the OSI model, a switch performs Layer 2 functions. Layer 2 is the Data Link Layer.

Several models of Ethernet switches are available to meet various user requirements. The Cisco Catalyst 2960 Series Ethernet switch is designed for the networks of medium-sized businesses and branch offices.

The Catalyst 2960 Series of switch are fixed-configuration, standalone devices that do not support modules or flash card slots. Because the physical configuration cannot change, fixed-configuration switches must be chosen based on the required number and type of ports. 2960 Series switches can provide 10/100 Fast Ethernet and 10/100/1000 Gigabit Ethernet connectivity. These switches use Cisco IOS software and can be configured using a GUI-based Cisco Network Assistant or through the CLI.

All switches support both half-duplex or full-duplex mode.

When a port is in half-duplex mode, at any given time, it can either send or receive data but not both. When a port is in full-duplex mode, it can simultaneously send and receive data, doubling the throughput.

Both the port and the connected device must be set to the same duplex mode. If they are not the same, a duplex mismatch occurs, which can lead to excessive collisions and degraded communication.

The speed and duplex can be set manually, or the switch port can use autonegotiation. Autonegotiation allows the switch to autodetect the speed and duplex of the device that is connected to the port. Autonegotiation is enabled by default on many Cisco switches.

For autonegotiation to be successful, both devices must support it. If the switch is in autonegotiation mode and the connected device does not support it, the switch uses the speed of the other device (10, 100, or 1000) and is set to half-duplex mode. Defaulting to half duplex can create problems if the non-autonegotiating device is set to full duplex.

If the connected device does not autonegotiate, manually configure the duplex settings on the switch to match the duplex settings on the connected device. The speed parameter can adjust itself, even if the connected port does not autonegotiate.

Switch settings, including the speed and duplex port parameters, can be configured using the Cisco IOS CLI. When configuring a switch using the Cisco IOS CLI, the interface and command structure is very similar to the Cisco routers.

As with the Cisco routers, there is a variety of choices for the Cisco IOS image for switches. The IP-base software image is supplied with the Cisco Catalyst 2960 switch. This image provides the switch with basic switching capabilities and IP services. Other Cisco IOS software images supply additional services to the IP-base image.

5.5.2 Power Up the Cisco 2960 Switch

Powering up a Cisco 2960 switch is similar to powering up a Cisco 1841 ISR.

The three basic steps for powering up a switch include:

Step 1. Check the components.

Step 2. Connect the cables to the switch.

Step 3. Power up the switch.

When the switch is on, the power-on self-test (POST) begins. During POST, the LEDs blink while a series of tests determine that the switch is functioning properly.

POST is completed when the SYST LED rapidly blinks green. If the switch fails POST, the SYST LED turns amber. When a switch fails POST, it is necessary to return the switch for repairs.

When all startup procedures are finished, the Cisco 2960 switch is ready to configure.

Lab Activity

Power up a Cisco 2960 switch.

5.5.3 Initial Switch Configuration

Refer to
Figure
in online course

There are several ways to configure and manage a Cisco LAN switch.

- Cisco Network Assistant

- Cisco Device Manager

- Cisco IOS CLI

- CiscoView Management Software

- *SNMP* Network Management Products

Some of these methods use IP connectivity or a web browser to connect to the switch, which requires an IP address. Unlike router interfaces, switch ports are not assigned IP addresses. To use an IP-based management product or Telnet session to manage a Cisco switch, it is necessary to configure a management IP address on the switch.

If the switch does not have an IP address, it is necessary to connect directly to the console port and use a terminal emulation program to perform configuration tasks.

Refer to
Figure
in online course

The Cisco Catalyst 2960 switch comes preconfigured and only needs to be assigned basic security information before being connected to the network.

The commands to configure the host name and passwords on the switch are the same commands used to configure the ISR. To use an IP-based management product or Telnet with a Cisco switch, configure a management IP address.

To assign an address to a switch, the address must be assigned to a virtual local area network *VLAN* interface. A VLAN allows multiple physical ports to be grouped together logically. By default, there is one VLAN, preconfigured in the switch, VLAN1, that provides access to management functions.

To configure the IP address assigned to the management interface on VLAN 1, enter global configuration mode.

```
Switch>enable
Switch#configure terminal
```

Next, enter the interface configuration mode for VLAN 1.

```
Switch(config)#interface vlan 1
```

Set the IP address, subnet mask, and default gateway for the management interface. The IP address must be valid for the local network where the switch is installed.

```
Switch(config-if)#ip address 192.168.1.2 255.255.255.0
 Switch(config-if)#exit
 Switch(config)#ip default-gateway 192.168.1.1
Switch(config)#end
```

Save the configuration by using the `copy running-configuration startup-configuration` command.

Refer to
Lab Activity
for this chapter

E-Lab Activity

Configure the basic settings on a Cisco Catalyst switch.

Refer to **Packet
Tracer Activity**
for this chapter

Packet Tracer Activity

Perform a basic switch configuration.

5.5.4 Connecting the LAN Switch to the Router

Refer to
Figure
in online course

Connect the Switch to the Network

To connect the switch to a router, use a straight-through cable. LED lights on the switch and router indicate that the connection is successful.

After the switch and router are connected, determine if the two devices are able to exchange messages.

First, check the IP address configuration. Use the **show running-configuration** command to verify that the IP address of the management interface on the switch VLAN 1 and the IP address of the directly connected router interface are on the same local network.

Then test the connection using the **ping** command. From the switch, ping the IP address of the directly connected router interface. Repeat the process from the router by pinging the management interface IP address assigned to the switch VLAN 1.

If the ping is not successful, verify the connections and configurations again. Check to ensure that all the cables are correct and that the connections are seated.

After the switch and router are successfully communicating, individual PCs can be connected to the switch using straight-through cables. These cables can be directly connected to the PCs, or can be used as part of the structured cabling leading to wall outlets.

Refer to
Figure
in online course

Switch ports can be an entry point to the network by unauthorized users. To prevent this, switches provide a feature called port security. Port security limits the number of valid MAC addresses allowed per port. The port does not forward packets with source MAC addresses that are outside the group of defined addresses.

There are three ways to configure port security.

Static

MAC addresses are manually assigned using the **switchport port-security mac-address** [*mac-address*] interface configuration command. Static MAC addresses are stored in the address table and added to the running configuration.

Dynamic

MAC addresses are dynamically learned and stored in the address table. The number of addresses learned can be controlled. By default, the maximum number of MAC addresses learned per port is one. Addresses that are learned are cleared from the table if the port is shutdown or if the switch is restarted.

Sticky

Similar to dynamic, except that the addresses are also saved to the running configuration.

Port security is disabled by default. If port security is enabled, a violation will result in the port being shutdown. For example, if dynamic port security is enabled and the maximum number of MAC addresses per port is one, the first address learned becomes the secure address. If another workstation attempts to access the port with a different MAC address, a security violation occurs.

There is a security violation when either of these situations occurs:

- The maximum number of secure MAC addresses has been added to the address table, and a device with a MAC address that is not in the address table attempts to access the interface.

- An address learned or configured on one secure interface is seen on another secure interface in the same VLAN.

Before port security can be activated, the port must be set to access mode with the **switchport mode access** command.

Refer to
Figure
in online course

To verify port security settings for the switch or the specified interface, use the **show port-security interface** interface-id command. The output displays the following:

- Maximum allowed number of secure MAC addresses for each interface

- Number of secure MAC addresses on the interface

- Number of security violations that have occurred

- Violation mode

Additionally, the **show port-security address** command displays the secure MAC addresses for all ports, and the **show port-security** command displays the port security settings for the switch.

If static port security or sticky port security is enabled, the **show running-config** command can be used to view the MAC address associated with a specific port. There are three ways to clear a learned MAC address that is saved in the running configuration:

- Use the **clear port-security sticky interface [port-number] access** to clear any learned addresses. Next, shutdown the port using the **shutdown** command. Finally, re-enable the port using the **no shutdown** command.

- Disable port security using the **no switchport port-security** interface command. Once disabled, re-enable port security.

- Reboot the switch.

Rebooting the switch will only work if the running configuration is not saved to the startup configuration file. If the running configuration is saved to the startup configuration file, that will eliminate the need for the switch to relearn addresses when the system reboots. However, the learned MAC address will always be associated with a particular port unless the port is cleared using the **clear port-security** command or disabling port security. If this is done, be sure to re-save the running configuration to the startup configuration file to prevent the switch from reverting to the original associated MAC address upon reboot.

If there are any ports on a switch that are unused, best practice is to disable them. It is simple to disable ports on a switch. Navigate to each unused port and issue the **shutdown** command. If a port needs to be activated, enter the **no shutdown** command on that interface.

In addition to enabling port security and shutting down unused ports, other security configurations on a switch include setting passwords on vty ports, enabling login banners, and encrypting passwords with the **service password-encryption** command. For these configurations, use the same Cisco IOS CLI commands as those used to configure a router.

Refer to **Packet Tracer Activity** for this chapter

Packet Tracer Activity

Configure and connect the switch to the LAN using a configuration checklist.

Refer to **Lab Activity** for this chapter

Lab Activity

Configure and connect the Cisco 2960 switch.

5.5.5 Cisco Discovery Protocol

Refer to
Figure
in online course

Cisco Discovery Protocol (CDP) is an information-gathering tool used on a switch, ISR, or router to share information with other directly connected Cisco devices. By default, CDP begins running when the device boots up. It then sends periodic messages, known as CDP advertisements, onto its directly connected networks.

CDP operates at Layer 2 only and can be used on many different types of local networks, including Ethernet and serial networks. Because it is a Layer 2 protocol, it can be used to determine the status of a directly connected link when no IP address has been configured, or if the IP address is incorrect.

Two Cisco devices that are directly connected on the same local network are referred to as being neighbors. The concept of neighbor devices is important to understand when interpreting the output of CDP commands.

Information gathered by CDP includes:

- Device identifiers - Configured host name

- Address list - Layer 3 address, if configured

- Port identifier - Directly connected port; for example, serial 0/0/0

- Capabilities list - Function or functions provided by the device

- Platform - Hardware platform of the device; for example, Cisco 1841

The output from the `show cdp neighbors` and `show cdp neighbors detail` commands displays the information that a Cisco device collects from its directly connected neighbors.

Viewing CDP information does not require logging in to the remote devices. Because CDP collects and displays a lot of information about directly connected neighbors, and no login is required, it is usually disabled in production networks for security purposes. Additionally, CDP consumes bandwidth and can impact network performance.

Refer to **Packet Tracer Activity** for this chapter

Packet Tracer Activity

Use the CDP show commands to discover information about devices in the network.

Chapter Summary

Chapter Quiz

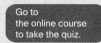
Go to
the online course
to take the quiz.

Take the chapter quiz to check your knowledge.

Your Chapter Notes

CHAPTER 6

Routing

Introduction

Refer to **Figure** in online course

6.1 Enabling Routing Protocols

Refer to **Figure** in online course

6.1.1 Routing Basics

As the internal network of an organization grows, it may be necessary to break up the network into multiple smaller networks for security or organizational purposes. This division is often accomplished by subnetting the network. Subnetting requires a router to pass traffic from one subnet to another.

To direct messages across networks so that they arrive at the correct destination, a router uses a table containing all the locally connected networks and the interfaces that are connected to each network. Each interface belongs to a different IP network.

A router determines which route, or path, to use by looking up the information stored in its routing table. The routing table also contains information about routes that the router can use to reach remote networks which are not locally attached.

Routes can be statically assigned to a router by an administrator, or routes can be dynamically given to the router by another router via a routing protocol.

Refer to **Figure** in online course

A router uses a routing table to determine where to send packets. The routing table contains a set of routes. Each route describes which gateway or interface the router uses to reach a specified network.

A route has four main components:

- Destination value
- Subnet mask
- Gateway or interface address
- *Route cost* or metric

When a router receives a packet, the router examines the destination IP address in that packet to determine where to forward the packet. The router then looks for a matching destination value in the routing table.

Each destination value within the route table refers to a destination network address. The destination IP address within a packet, however, consists of both a network address and a host address. For the router to determine if its table contains a route to the destination network, it must determine there is a match between the IP network address and one of the destination values in the routing table. This means the router must determine which bits of the IP address represent the network and which bits represent the host.

The router looks up the subnet mask assigned to each potential route in the table. The router applies each subnet mask to the destination IP address in the packet. The resulting network address is then compared to the network address of the route in the table. If a match is found, the packet is forwarded out the correct interface or to the appropriate gateway. If the network address matches more than one route in the routing table, the router uses the route that has the most specific, or longest, network address match.

Sometimes there is more than one route to the destination network. In this case, routing protocol rules determine which route the router uses.

If none of the route entries match, the router directs the message to the gateway specified by its default route, if a default route is configured. Otherwise, the packet is simply dropped.

Refer to **Figure** in online course

On a Cisco router, the Cisco IOS command `show ip route` displays the routes in the routing table. Several types of routes can appear in the routing table.

Directly Connected Routes

When the router powers up, the configured interfaces are enabled. As the interfaces become operational, the router stores the directly attached, local-network addresses as connected routes in the routing table. On Cisco routers, these routes are identified in the routing table with the prefix C. The routes are automatically updated whenever the interface is reconfigured or shut down.

Static Routes

A network administrator can manually configure a static route to a specific network. A static route does not change until the administrator manually reconfigures it. These routes are identified in the routing table with the prefix S.

Dynamically Updated Routes (Dynamic Routes)

Dynamic routes are automatically created and maintained by routing protocols. Routing protocols exchange routing information with other routers in the network. Dynamically updated routes are identified in the routing table with the prefix that corresponds to the type of routing protocol that created the route. For example, R is used for the Routing Information Protocol (*RIP*).

Default Route

The default route is a type of static route that specifies the gateway to use when the routing table does not contain a path for the destination network. It is common for default routes to point to the next router in the path to the ISP. If a subnet has only one router, that router is automatically the default gateway, because all network traffic to and from that local network has no option but to travel through that router.

Routing tables do not contain end-to-end information about the entire path from a source network to a destination network. They only contain information about the next hop along that path. The next hop is typically a directly-connected network within the routing table.

In the case of a static route, the next hop could be any IP address, as long as it is reachable by that router. Eventually the message gets passed to a router that is directly connected to the destination host and the message is delivered. Routing information between all the intermediate routers on a path is in the form of network addresses not specific hosts. It is only in the final router that the destination address in the routing table points specifically to a host computer rather than a network.

Refer to **Figure** in online course

Configuring Static Routes

Static routes are manually configured by a network administrator. Configuring a static route on a Cisco router requires these steps:

Step 1. Connect to the router using a console cable.

Step 2. Open a HyperTerminal window to connect with the first router that you want to configure.

Step 3. Enter privileged mode by typing **enable** at the **R1>** prompt. Note how the > symbol changes to a # to indicate that privilege mode is being used.

```
R1>enable
R1#
```

Step 4. Enter global configuration mode.

```
R1#config terminal
R1(config)#
```

Step 5. Use the **ip route** Cisco IOS command to configure the static route, with the following format.

ip route [*destination_network*] [*subnet_mask*] [*gateway_address*]

or

ip route [*destination_network*] [*subnet_mask*] [*exit_interface*]

For example, to enable router 1 (R1) to reach a host on network 192.168.16.0, the administrator configures a static route on R1 with the following Cisco IOS command in global configuration mode:

```
R1(config)#ip route 192.168.16.0 255.255.255.0 192.168.15.1
```

or

```
R1(config)#ip route 192.168.16.0 255.255.255.0 S0/0/0
```

To enable two-way communication with a host on network 192.168.16.0, the administrator also configures a static route on router 2 (R2).

Because static routes are configured manually, network administrators must add and delete static routes to reflect any changes in network topology. On small networks, static routes require very little maintenance because there are not many possible changes. In a large network, manually maintaining routing tables could require significant administrative time. For this reason, larger networks generally use dynamic routing rather than static routes.

Refer to Packet Tracer Activity for this chapter

Packet Tracer Activity

Manually configure and reconfigure static routes.

6.1.2 Routing Protocols

Refer to Figure in online course

Routes can change very quickly. Problems with cables and hardware failures can make destinations unreachable through the designated interface. Routers need to be able to quickly update routes in a way that does not depend on the administrator to make the changes manually.

Routers use routing protocols to dynamically manage information received from their own interfaces and from other routers. Routing protocols can also be configured to manage manually entered routes.

Dynamic routing makes it possible to avoid the time-consuming process of configuring static routes. Dynamic routing enables routers to react to changes in the network and to adjust their routing tables accordingly, without the intervention of the network administrator.

A dynamic routing protocol learns all the available routes, places the best routes into the routing table, and removes routes when they are no longer valid. The method that a routing protocol uses to determine the best route is called a *routing algorithm*. There are two main classes of routing algorithms: *distance vector* and *link state*. Each type uses a different method for determining the best route to a destination network.

Whenever the topology of a network changes because of reconfiguration or failure, the routing tables in all the routers must also change to reflect an accurate view of the new topology. When all the routers in a network have updated their tables to reflect the new route, the routers are said to have converged.

The specific routing algorithm that is being used is a very important factor in dynamic routing. For two routers to exchange routes, they must be using the same routing protocol and therefore the same routing algorithm.

Refer to
Figure
in online course

The distance vector routing algorithm periodically passes copies of the routing table from router to router. These regular updates between routers communicate topology changes.

The distance vector algorithm evaluates the route information it receives from other routers using two basic criteria:

- Distance - How far away is the network from this router?

- Vector - In which direction should the packet be sent to reach this network?

The distance component of a route is expressed in terms of a route cost, or metric, that can be based on the following items:

- Number of hops

- Administrative cost

- Bandwidth

- Transmission speed

- Likelihood of delays

- Reliability

The vector, or direction, component of a route is the address of the next hop along the path to the network named in the route.

An analogy for distance vectors are the highway signs found at intersections. A sign points toward a destination and indicates the distance that must be traveled to reach that destination. Further down the highway, another sign points toward the same destination, but now the distance remaining to that destination is shorter. As long as the distance is shorter, the traffic is on the best path.

Refer to
Figure
in online course

Each router that uses distance vector routing communicates its routing information to its neighbors. Neighbor routers share a directly connected network. The interface that leads to each directly connected network has a distance of 0.

Each router receives a routing table from its neighbor routers. For example, R2 receives information from R1. R2 adds to the metric, in this case the *hop count*, to show that there is now one more hop to get to the destination network. Then R2 sends this new routing table to its neighbors, including R3. This step-by-step process occurs in all directions between neighbor routers.

Eventually, each router learns about other more-remote networks based on the information that it receives from its neighbors. Each of the network entries in the routing table has an accumulated distance vector to show how far away that network is in a given direction.

As the distance vector discovery process continues, routers discover the best path to destination networks based on the information they receive from each neighbor. The best path is the path with the shortest distance or smallest metric.

Routing table updates also occur when the topology changes, for example, when a new network is added or when a router fails, causing a network to become unreachable. As with the network discovery process, topology change updates proceed step-by-step by sending copies of routing tables from router to router.

Refer to
Interactive Graphic
in online course.

Activity

For each router select the shortest path, based on the number of hops, to the destination Ethernet networks. If the network is directly connected, specify the exit interface; otherwise, specify the next hop router.

Click each router to complete the routing table entries. To proceed to another router, first click Check, and then click the new router.

Refer to
Lab Activity
for this chapter

Lab Activity

Create a network topology diagram based on the output of the `show ip route` command.

6.1.3 Common Interior Routing Protocols

Refer to
Figure
in online course

Routing Information Protocol (RIP) is a distance vector routing protocol that is used in thousands of networks throughout the world. It was initially specified in RFC 1058.

Characteristics of RIP include:

- Is a distance vector routing protocol
- Uses hop count as the *metric* for path selection
- Defines a hop count greater than 15 as an unreachable route
- Sends routing table contents every 30 seconds

When a router receives a routing update with a change, it updates its routing table to reflect that change. If the router learns a new route from another router, it increases the hop count value by one before adding that route to its own routing table. The router uses the local network address of the directly connected router that sent the update as the next hop address.

After updating its routing table, the router immediately begins transmitting routing updates to inform other network routers of the change. These updates, called *triggered update*s, are sent independently of the regularly scheduled updates that RIP routers forward.

Refer to
Figure
in online course

Routing Information Protocol (RIP)

RIP is simple and easy to implement. These advantages make RIP a widely used and popular routing protocol.

RIP has several disadvantages:

- Allows a maximum of 15 hops, so it can only be used for networks that connect no more than 16 routers in a series.

- Periodically sends complete copies of the entire routing table to directly connected neighbors. In a large network, this can cause a significant amount of network traffic each time there is an update.

- Converges slowly on larger networks when the network changes.

There are currently two versions of RIP available: RIPv1 and RIPv2. RIPv2 has many advantages over RIPv1 and is usually used unless the equipment cannot support RIPv2. The most significant difference between RIP versions 1 and 2 is that RIPv2 can support classless routing, because it includes the subnet mask information in routing updates. RIPv1 does not send subnet mask information in the updates; therefore, it must rely on the classful default subnet masks.

Enhanced Interior Gateway Routing Protocol (EIGRP)

Refer to
Figure
in online course

EIGRP is a Cisco-proprietary, enhanced distance vector routing protocol. EIGRP was developed to address some of the limitations of other distance vector routing protocols, such as RIP. These limitations include the use of the hop count metric and the maximum network size of 15 hops.

EIGRP uses a number of metrics, including a configured bandwidth value and the delay encountered when a packet travels a particular route.

The characteristics of EIGRP are:

- Uses a variety of metrics to calculate the cost of a route

- Combines the next hop and metric features of distance vector protocols with additional database and update features

- Has a maximum hop count of 224 hops

Unlike RIP, EIGRP does not rely only on the routing table in the router to hold all the information it needs to operate. EIGRP creates two additional database tables: the neighbor table and the topology table.

The neighbor table stores data about the neighboring routers that are on directly connected local networks. This neighbor table includes information such as the interface IP addresses, interface type, and bandwidth.

EIGRP builds the topology table from each of the advertisements of its neighbors. The topology table contains all the routes advertised by the neighbor routers. EIGRP depends on a routing algorithm called Diffused Update Algorithm (*DUAL*) to calculate the shortest path to a destination within a network and to install this route into the routing table. The topology table enables a router running EIGRP to find the best alternate path quickly when a network change occurs. If no alternate route exists in the topology table, EIGRP queries its neighbors to find a new path to the destination.

Unlike RIP, which is limited to small simple networks of less than 15 hops, EIGRP is ideal for larger, more complex networks up to 224 hops in size that require fast convergence.

Refer to
Figure
in online course

Link-state Protocol

Routers that use the distance vector routing algorithm have little information about distant networks and none about distant routers. The link-state routing algorithm maintains a full database of distant routers and how they interconnect.

Link-state routing uses the following features:

- Routing table - List of the known paths and interfaces.

- Link-state advertisement (*LSA*) - Small packet of routing information that is sent between routers. LSAs describe the state of the interfaces (links) of a router and other information, such as the IP address of each link.

- *Topological database* - Collection of information gathered from all the LSAs received by the router.

- Shortest Path First (*SPF*) algorithm - Calculation performed on the database that results in the SPF tree. The SPF tree is a map of the network as seen from the point of view of the router. The information in this tree is used to build the routing table.

When LSAs are received from other routers, the SPF algorithm analyzes the information in the database to construct the SPF tree. Based on the SPF tree, the SPF algorithm then calculates the shortest paths to other networks. Each time a new LSA packet causes a change to the link-state database, SPF recalculates the best paths and updates the routing table.

OSPF

Refer to **Figure** in online course

Open Shortest Path First (*OSPF*) is a non-proprietary, link-state routing protocol described in RFC 2328. The characteristics of OSPF are:

- Uses the SPF algorithm to calculate the lowest cost to a destination

- Sends routing updates only when the topology changes; does not send periodic updates of the entire routing table

- Provides fast convergence

- Supports Variable Length Subnet Mask (VLSM) and discontiguous subnets

- Provides route authentication

In OSPF networks, routers send link-state advertisements to each other when a change occurs, for example, when a new neighbor is added, or when a link fails or is restored.

If the network topology changes, the routers affected by the change send update LSAs to the rest of the network. All routers update their topology databases accordingly, regenerate their SPF trees to find new shortest paths to each network, and update their routing tables with the changed routes.

OSPF requires more router resources, such as RAM and CPU processing power, and is an advanced networking protocol that requires an experienced support staff.

6.1.4 Routing Within an Organization

Refer to **Figure** in online course

Each routing protocol uses different metrics. The metric used by one routing protocol is not comparable to the metric used by another routing protocol. Two routing protocols might choose different paths to the same destination because they use different metrics. For example, RIP chooses the path with the fewest number of hops, whereas EIGRP chooses the path based on the highest bandwidth and least delay.

Metrics used in IP routing protocols include:

- Hop count - Number of routers a packet must traverse.

- Bandwidth - Bandwidth of a specific link.

- Load - Traffic utilization of a specific link.

- Delay - Time a packet takes to traverse a path.

- Reliability — Probability of a link failure, based on the interface error count or previous link failures.

- Cost - Determined by either the Cisco IOS application or the network administrator to indicate preference for a route. Cost can represent a metric, a combination of metrics, or a policy.

It is possible to have more than one routing protocol enabled on a single router. Additionally, a network administrator may choose to configure static routes to a specific destination. If a router has two different paths to a destination based on two different routing protocols and their metrics, how does the router know which path to use?

The router uses what is known as the administrative distance (*AD*). The AD represents the "trust-worthiness" of the route. The lower the AD, the more the trustworthy the route. For example, a static route has an AD of 1, whereas a RIP-discovered route has an AD of 120. Given two separate routes to the same destination, the router chooses the route with the lowest AD. When a router has the choice of a static route and a RIP route, the static route takes precedence. Additionally, a directly connected route with an AD of 0 takes precedence over a static route with an AD of 1.

Refer to
Figure
in online course

Sometimes it is necessary to use multiple routing protocols, for example, when merging two pre-existing networks. However, when initially designing a network, it is recommended that only one routing protocol be enabled for the entire network. Having one protocol makes it easier to support and troubleshoot the network. Deciding which type of routing protocol to select can be difficult even for expert network designers.

Small networks with only one gateway to the Internet can probably use static routes. Such a topology rarely needs dynamic routing.

As an organization grows and adds routers to its network topology, RIPv2 can be used. It is easy to configure and works well in small networks. When a network begins to exceed 15 routers, RIP is no longer a good choice.

For larger networks, EIGRP and OSPF are commonly used, but there is no simple principle that makes it obvious to choose one over the other. Each network has to be considered independently. The three main criteria to consider are:

- *Ease of management* - What information does the protocol keep about itself? Which `show` commands are available?

- *Ease of configuration* - How many commands does the average configuration require? Is it possible to configure several routers in the network with the same configuration?

- *Efficiency* - How much bandwidth does the routing protocol use while it is in a steady state, and how much could it use when converging in response to a major network event?

6.1.5 Configuring and Verifying RIP

Refer to
Figure
in online course

RIP is a popular distance vector protocol supported by most routers. It is an appropriate choice for small networks containing multiple routers. Before configuring RIP on a router, think about the networks a router serves, and the interfaces on the router that connect to these networks.

The figure shows three routers. Each router serves a separate private local network, so there are three LANs. The routers are also connected by separate networks, so there are a total of six networks shown.

With this topology, R1 does not automatically know how to reach the 10.0.0.0/8 network, or the 192.168.4.0/24 network. R1 is only able to reach those networks after RIP routing is properly configured. Once RIP routing is configured, R2 and R3 will forward routing updates to R1 containing information on the availability of the 10.0.0.0/8 and 192.168.4.0/24 networks.

Before configuring RIP, assign an IP address and enable all the physical interfaces that will participate in routing.

For the most basic RIPv2 configuration, there are three commands to remember:

```
Router(config)#router rip
 Router (config-router)#version 2
Router(config-router)#network [network_number]
```

Enter the `router rip` command in global configuration mode to enable RIP on the router. Enter the `network` command from router configuration mode to tell the router which networks are part of

Refer to **Figure** in online course

the RIP routing process. The routing process associates specific interfaces with the network numbers specified, and begins to send and receive RIP updates on these interfaces.

After a configuration is done, it is a good idea to compare the running configuration with an accurate topology diagram to verify the network numbers and interface IP addresses. This is good practice because it is easy to make a simple data entry error.

There are several ways to verify that RIP is functioning properly in the network. One way to verify that routing is working properly is to ping devices on remote networks. If the ping is successful, it is likely that routing is working.

Another method is to run the IP routing verification commands `show ip protocols` and `show ip route` at the CLI prompt.

The `show ip protocols` command verifies that RIP routing is configured, that the correct interfaces are sending and receiving RIP updates, and that the router is advertising the correct networks.

The `show ip route` command shows the routing table, which verifies that routes received by RIP neighbors are installed in the routing table.

The `debug ip rip` command can be used to observe the networks advertised in the routing updates as they are sent and received. Debug commands display router activity in real time. Because debug activity uses router processor resources, debugging should be used with care in a production network, because it can affect network operation.

Refer to **Packet Tracer Activity** for this chapter

Packet Tracer Activity

Configure and verify RIP.

Refer to **Lab Activity** for this chapter

Lab Activity

Configure and verify RIP.

6.2 Exterior Routing Protocols

6.2.1 Autonomous Systems

Refer to **Figure** in online course

The Internet routing architecture has evolved over the years into a distributed system of interconnected networks. The Internet is now so vast and involves so many networks that it is impossible for a single organization to manage all the routing information needed to reach every destination around the world.

Instead, the Internet is divided up into collections of networks called Autonomous Systems (*AS*), which are independently controlled by different organizations and companies.

An AS is a set of networks controlled by a single administrative authority using the same internal routing policy throughout. Each AS is identified by a unique AS number (*ASN*). ASNs are controlled and registered on the Internet.

The most common example of an AS is the ISP. Most businesses connect to the Internet through an ISP, and so become part of the routing domain of that ISP. The AS is administered by the ISP and, therefore, not only includes its own network routes but also manages the routes to all the business and other customer networks that are connected to it.

Refer to **Figure** in online course

The same ASN applies to all network devices within the AS routing domain.

ISP A is an AS whose routing domain includes a local business that directly connects to that ISP for Internet access. The business does not have a separate ASN. Instead, it uses the ASN of ISP A (ASN 100) in its routing information.

Also shown is a large global business with corporate offices located in Hong Kong and New York. Because they are located in different countries, each office connects to a different local ISP for Internet access. This means that the business is connected to two ISPs. Which AS does it belong to and which ASN does it use?

Because the company communicates through both ISP B and ISP C, this causes routing confusion in terms of connectivity. Traffic from the internet does not know which AS to use to reach the large global business. To solve the problem, the business registers as an AS in its own right and is assigned an ASN of 400.

Refer to
Interactive Graphic
in online course.

Activity

Identify which networks belong to which Autonomous Systems.

For each scenario, select either Uses ASN of ISP or Uses Private ASN.

6.2.2 Routing Across the Internet

Refer to
Figure
in online course

Interior Gateway Protocols (*IGP*s) are used to exchange routing information within an AS or individual organization. The purpose of an interior routing protocol is to find the best path through the internal network. IGPs run on the routers inside an organization. Examples of IGPs are RIP, EIGRP, and OSPF.

By contrast, exterior gateway protocols (*EGP*s) are designed to exchange routing information between different autonomous systems. Because each AS is managed by a different administration and may use different interior protocols, networks must use a protocol that can communicate between diverse systems. The EGP serves as a translator for ensuring that external routing information gets successfully interpreted inside each AS network.

EGPs run on the exterior routers. These are the routers that are located at the border of an AS. Exterior routers are also called border gateways, or boundary routers.

Unlike interior routers, which exchange individual routes with each other using IGPs, exterior routers exchange information about how to reach various networks using exterior protocols. Exterior routing protocols seek to find the best path through the Internet as a sequence of autonomous systems.

The most common exterior routing protocol on the Internet today is Border Gateway Protocol (*BGP*). It is estimated that 95% of autonomous systems use BGP. The most current version of BGP is version 4 (BGP-4), for which the latest description is provided in RFC 4271.

Refer to
Figure
in online course

Each AS is responsible for informing other autonomous systems about which networks they can reach through that AS. Autonomous systems exchange this *reachability information* with each other through exterior routing protocols that run on dedicated routers called border gateways.

Packets are routed across the Internet in several steps.

1. The source host sends a packet destined for a remote host located in another AS.

2. Because the destination IP address of the packet is not a local network, the interior routers keep passing the packet along their default routes, until eventually it arrives at an exterior router at the edge of the local AS.

3. The exterior router maintains a database for all the autonomous systems with which it connects. This *reachability* database tells the router that the path to the destination network passes through several autonomous systems, and that the next hop on the path is through a directly connected exterior router on a neighboring AS.

4. The exterior router directs the packet to its next hop on the path, which is the exterior router at the neighboring AS.

5. The packet arrives at the neighboring AS, where the exterior router checks its own reachability database and forwards the packet to the next AS on the path.

6. The process is repeated at each AS until the exterior router at the destination AS recognizes the destination IP address of the packet as an internal network in that AS.

7. The final exterior router then directs the packet to the next hop interior router listed in its routing table. From then on, the packet is treated just like any local packet and is directed through interior routing protocols through a series of internal next hops until it arrives at the destination host.

6.2.3 Exterior Routing Protocols and the ISP

Refer to
Figure
in online course

EGPs provide many useful features for ISPs. Exterior protocols allow traffic to be routed across the Internet to remote destinations. They also provide the method by which ISPs can set and enforce policies and local preferences so that the traffic flow through the ISP is efficient and that none of the internal routes are overloaded with *transit traffic*.

Business customers insist on reliability for their Internet service. ISPs must make sure that the Internet connection for those customers is always available. They do this by providing backup routes and routers in case the regular route fails. During normal conditions, the ISP advertises the regular route to other autonomous systems. If that regular route fails, the ISP sends an exterior protocol update message to advertise the backup route instead.

Refer to
Figure
in online course

The flow of messages in the Internet is called traffic. Internet traffic can be categorized in one of two ways:

- *Local traffic* - Traffic carried within an AS that either originated in that same AS, or is intended to be delivered within that AS. This is like local traffic on a street.

- Transit traffic - Traffic that was generated outside that AS and can travel through the internal AS network to be delivered to destinations outside the AS. This is like through traffic on a street.

The flow of traffic between autonomous systems is carefully controlled. It is important to be able to limit or even prohibit certain types of messages from going to or from an AS for security reasons or to prevent overloading.

Many autonomous systems network administrators choose not to carry transit traffic. Transit traffic can cause routers to overload and fail if those routers do not have the capacity to handle large amounts of traffic.

6.2.4 Configuring and Verifying BGP

Refer to
Figure
in online course

When an ISP puts a router at a customer location, they usually configure it with a default static route to the ISP. Sometimes, an ISP may want the router to be included in its AS and to participate in BGP. In these instances, it is necessary to configure the customer premise router with the commands necessary to enable BGP.

The first step in enabling BGP on a router is to configure the AS number. This step is done with the command:

```
router bgp [AS_number]
```

The next step is to identify the ISP router that is the BGP neighbor with which the customer premises equipment (CPE) router exchanges information. The command to identify the neighbor router is:

neighbor [*IP_address*] **remote-as** [*AS_number*]

When an ISP customer has its own registered IP address block, it may want the routes to some of its internal networks to be known on the Internet. To use BGP to advertise an internal route, the network address needs to be identified. The format of the command is:

network [*network_address*]

When the CPE is installed and the routing protocols are configured, the customer has both local and Internet connectivity. Now the customer is able to fully participate in other services that the ISP offers.

The IP addresses used for BGP are normally registered, routable addresses that identify unique organizations. In very large organizations, private addresses may be used in the BGP process. On the Internet, BGP should never be used to advertise a private network address.

Lab Activity

Refer to **Lab Activity** for this chapter

Configure BGP on the external gateway router.

Chapter Summary

Click through the buttons for summary information.

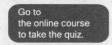

Chapter Quiz

Take the chapter quiz to check your knowledge.

Your Chapter Notes

CHAPTER 7

ISP Services

Introduction

Refer to
Figure
in online course

7.1 Introducing ISP Services

Refer to
Figure
in online course

7.1.1 Customer Requirements

After the connection is made to the ISP, the business or customer must decide which services they need from the ISP.

ISPs serve several markets. Individuals in homes make up the consumer market. Large, multinational companies make up the enterprise market. In between are smaller markets, such as small- to medium-sized businesses, or larger nonprofit organizations. Each of these customers have different service requirements.

Escalating customer expectations and increasingly competitive markets are forcing ISPs to offer new services. These services enable the ISPs to increase revenue and to differentiate themselves from their competitors.

Email, web hosting, media streaming, IP telephony, and file transfer are important services that ISPs can provide to all customers. These services are critical for the ISP consumer market and for the small- to medium-sized business that does not have the expertise to maintain their own services.

Refer to
Figure
in online course

Many organizations, both large and small, find it expensive to keep up with new technologies, or they simply prefer to devote resources to other parts of the business. ISPs offer managed services that enable these organizations to have access to the leading network technologies and applications without having to make large investments in equipment and support.

When a company subscribes to a managed service, the service provider manages the network equipment and applications according to the terms of a service level agreement (SLA). Some managed services are also hosted, meaning that the service provider hosts the applications in its facility instead of at the customer site.

The following are three scenarios that describe different ISP customer relationships:

- *Scenario 1* - The customer owns and manages all their own network equipment and services. These customers only need reliable Internet connectivity from the ISP.

- *Scenario 2* - The ISP provides Internet connectivity. The ISP also owns and manages the network connecting equipment installed at the customer site. ISP responsibilities include setting up, maintaining, and administering the equipment for the customer. The customer is responsible for monitoring the status of the network and the applications, and receives regular reports on the performance of the network.

■ *Scenario 3 -* The customer owns the network equipment, but the applications that the business relies on are hosted by the ISP. The actual servers that run the applications are located at the ISP facility. These servers may be owned by the customer or the ISP, although the ISP maintains both the servers and the applications. Servers are normally kept in *server farm*s in the ISP network operations center (NOC), and are connected to the ISP network with a high-speed switch.

7.1.2 Reliability and Availability

Refer to
Figure
in online course

Creating new services can be challenging. Not only must ISPs understand what their customers want, but they must have the ability and the resources to provide those services. As business and Internet applications become more complex, an increasing number of ISP customers rely on the services provided or managed by the ISP.

ISPs provide services to customers for a fee and guarantee a level of service in the SLA. To meet customer expectations, the service offerings have to be reliable and available.

Reliability

Reliability can be measured in two ways: mean time between failure (*MTBF*) and mean time to repair *MTTR*. Equipment manufacturers specify MTBF based on tests they perform as part of manufacturing. The measure of equipment robustness is fault tolerance. The longer the MTBF, the greater the fault tolerance. MTTR is established by warranty or service agreements.

When there is an equipment failure, and the network or service becomes unavailable, it impacts the ability of the ISP to meet the terms of the SLA. To prevent this, an ISP may purchase expensive service agreements for critical hardware to ensure rapid manufacturer or vendor response. An ISP may also choose to purchase redundant hardware and keep spare parts on site.

Availability

Availability is normally measured in the percentage of time that a resource is accessible. A perfect availability percentage is 100%, meaning that the system is never down or unreachable. Traditionally, telephone services are expected to be available 99.999% of the time. This is called the five-9s standard of availability. With this standard, only a very small percentage (0.001%) of downtime is acceptable. As ISPs offer more critical business services, such as IP telephony or high-volume retail sale transactions, ISPs must meet the higher expectations of their customers. ISPs ensure accessibility by doubling up on network devices and servers using technologies designed for high availability. In redundant configurations, if one device fails, the other one can take over the functions automatically.

7.2 Protocols That Support ISP Services

7.2.1 Review of TCP/IP Protocols

Refer to
Figure
in online course

Today, ISP customers are using mobile phones as televisions, PCs as telephones, and televisions as interactive gaming stations with many different entertainment options. As network services become more advanced, ISPs must accommodate these customer preferences. The development of converged IP networks enables all of these services to be delivered over a common network.

To provide support for the multiple end-user applications that rely on TCP/IP for delivery, it is important for the ISP support personnel to be familiar with the operation of the TCP/IP protocols.

ISP servers need to be able to support multiple applications for many different customers. For this support, they must use functions provided by the two TCP/IP transport protocols, TCP and UDP. Common hosted applications, like web serving and email accounts, also depend on underlying TCP/IP protocols to ensure their reliable delivery. In addition, all IP services rely on domain name servers, hosted by the ISPs, to provide the link between the IP addressing structure and the URLs that customers use to access them.

Refer to **Figure** in online course

Clients and servers use specific protocols and standards when exchanging information. The TCP/IP protocols can be represented using a four-layer model. Many of the services provided to ISP customers depend on protocols that reside at the Application and Transport layers of the TCP/IP model.

Application Layer Protocols

Application Layer protocols specify the format and control the information necessary for many of the common Internet communication functions. Among these protocols are:

- Domain Name System (*DNS*) - Resolves Internet names to IP addresses.

- HyperText Transfer Protocol (HTTP) -Transfers files that make up the web pages of the World Wide Web.

- Simple Mail Transfer Protocol (SMTP) - Transfers mail messages and attachments.

- Telnet - Terminal emulation protocol that provides remote access to servers and networking devices.

- File Transfer Protocol (FTP) - Transfers files between systems interactively.

Transport Layer Protocols

Different types of data can have unique requirements. For some applications, communication segments must arrive in a specific sequence to be processed successfully. In other instances, all the data must be received for any of it to be of use. Sometimes, an application can tolerate the loss of a small amount of data during transmission over the network.

In today's converged networks, applications with very different transport needs may be communicating on the same network. Different Transport Layer protocols have different rules to enable devices to handle these diverse data requirements.

Additionally, the lower layers are not aware that there are multiple applications sending data on the network. Their responsibility is to get the data to the device. It is the job of the Transport Layer to deliver the data to the appropriate application.

The two primary Transport Layer protocols are TCP and UDP.

Refer to **Figure** in online course

The TCP/IP model and the OSI model have similarities and differences.

Similarities

- Use of layers to visualize the interaction of protocols and services

- Comparable Transport and Network layers

- Used in the networking field when referring to protocol interaction

Differences

- OSI model breaks the function of the TCP/IP Application Layer into distinct layers. The upper three layers of the OSI model specify the same functionality as the Application Layer of the TCP/IP model.

- The TCP/IP suite does not specify protocols for the physical network interconnection. The two lower layers of the OSI model are concerned with access to the physical network and the delivery of bits between hosts on a local network.

The TCP/IP model is based on actual developed protocols and standards, whereas the OSI model is a theoretical guide for how protocols interact.

7.2.2 Transport Layer Protocols

Refer to
Figure
in online course

Different applications have different transport needs. There are two protocols at the Transport Layer: TCP and UDP.

TCP

TCP is a reliable, guaranteed-delivery protocol. TCP specifies the methods hosts use to acknowledge the receipt of packets, and requires the source host to resend packets that are not acknowledged. TCP also governs the exchange of messages between the source and destination hosts to create a communication session. TCP is often compared to a pipeline, or a *persistent connection*, between hosts. Because of this, TCP is referred to as a *connection-oriented* protocol.

TCP requires overhead, which includes extra bandwidth and increased processing, to keep track of the individual conversations between the source and destination hosts and to process acknowledgements and retransmissions. In some cases, the delays caused by this overhead cannot be tolerated by the application. These applications are better suited for UDP.

UDP

UDP is a very simple, *connectionless* protocol. It provides low overhead data delivery. UDP is considered a "best effort" Transport Layer protocol because it does not provide error checking, guaranteed data delivery, or flow control. Because UDP is a "best effort" protocol, UDP datagrams may arrive at the destination out of order, or may even be lost all together. Applications that use UDP can tolerate small amounts of missing data. An example of a UDP application is Internet radio. If a piece of data is not delivered, there may only be a minor effect on the quality of the *broadcast*.

Refer to
Figure
in online course

Applications, such as databases, web pages, and email, need to have all data arrive at the destination in its original condition, for the data to be useful. Any missing data can cause the messages to be corrupt or unreadable. These applications are designed to use a Transport Layer protocol that implements reliability. The additional network overhead required to provide this reliability is considered a reasonable cost for successful communication.

The Transport Layer protocol is determined by the type of application data being sent. For example, an email message requires acknowledged delivery and therefore would use TCP. An email client, using SMTP, sends an email message as a stream of *byte*s to the Transport Layer. At the Transport Layer, the TCP functionality divides the stream into segments.

Within each segment, TCP identifies each byte, or octet, with a sequence number. These segments are passed to the Internet Layer, which places each segment in a packet for transmission. This process is known as encapsulation. At the destination, the process is reversed, and the packets are de-encapsulated. The enclosed segments are sent through the TCP process, which converts the segments back to a stream of bytes to be passed to the email server application.

Refer to
Figure
in online course

Before a TCP session can be used, the source and destination hosts exchange messages to set up the connection over which data segments can be sent. The two hosts use a three step process to set up the connection.

In the first step, the source host sends a type of message, called a Synchronization Message, or SYN, to begin the TCP session establishment process. The message serves two purposes:

- It indicates the intention of the source host to establish a connection with the destination host over which to send the data.

- It synchronizes the TCP sequence numbers between the two hosts, so that each host can keep track of the segments sent and received during the conversation.

For the second step, the destination host replies to the SYN message with a synchronization acknowledgement, or SYN-ACK, message.

In the last step, the sending host receives the SYN-ACK and it sends an *ACK* message back to complete the connection setup. Data segments can now be reliably sent.

This SYN, SYN-ACK, ACK activity between the TCP processes on the two hosts is called a *three-way handshake*.

Refer to **Figure** in online course

When a host sends message segments to a destination host using TCP, the TCP process on the source host starts a timer. The timer allows sufficient time for the message to reach the destination host and for an acknowledgement to be returned. If the source host does not receive an acknowledgement from the destination within the allotted time, the timer expires, and the source assumes the message is lost. The portion of the message that was not acknowledged is then re-sent.

In addition to acknowledgement and retransmission, TCP also specifies how messages are reassembled at the destination host. Each TCP segment contains a sequence number. At the destination host, the TCP process stores received segments in a buffer. By evaluating the segment sequence numbers, the TCP process can confirm that there are no gaps in the received data. When data is received out of order, TCP can also reorder the segments as necessary.

7.2.3 Differences Between TCP and UDP

Refer to **Figure** in online course

UDP is a very simple protocol. Because it is not connection-oriented and does not provide the sophisticated retransmission, sequencing, and flow control mechanisms of TCP, UDP has a much lower overhead.

UDP is often referred to as an unreliable delivery protocol, because there is no guarantee that a message has been received by the destination host. This does not mean that applications that use UDP are unreliable. It simply means that these functions are not provided by the Transport Layer protocol and must be implemented elsewhere if required.

Although the total amount of UDP traffic found on a typical network is often relatively low, Application Layer protocols that do use UDP include:

- Domain Name System (DNS)

- Simple Network Management Protocol (SNMP)

- Dynamic Host Configuration Protocol (DHCP)

- RIP routing protocol

- Trivial File Transfer Protocol (TFTP)

- Online games

Refer to **Figure** in online course

The main differences between TCP and UDP are the specific functions that each protocol implements and the amount of overhead incurred. Viewing the headers of both protocols is an easy way to see the differences between them.

Each TCP segment has 20 bytes of overhead in the header that encapsulates the Application Layer data. This overhead is incurred because of the error-checking mechanisms supported by TCP.

The pieces of communication in UDP are called datagrams. These datagrams are sent as "best effort" and, therefore, only require 8 bytes of overhead.

Refer to
Interactive Graphic
in online course.

Activity

Identify the characteristics and protocols of TCP and UDP.

Drag the option to either TCP or UDP.

7.2.4 Supporting Multiple Services

Refer to
Figure
in online course

The task of managing multiple simultaneous communication processes is done at the Transport Layer. The TCP and UDP services keep track of the various applications that are communicating over the network. To differentiate the segments and datagrams for each application, both TCP and UDP have header fields that can uniquely identify these applications for data communications purposes.

A source port and destination port are located in the header of each segment or datagram. Port numbers are assigned in various ways, depending on whether the message is a request or a response. When a client application sends a request to a server application, the destination port contained in the header is the port number that is assigned to the application running on the server. For example, when a web browser application makes a request to a web server, the browser uses TCP and port number 80. This is because TCP port 80 is the default port assigned to web-serving applications. Many common applications have default port assignments. Email servers that are using SMTP are usually assigned to TCP port 25.

As segments are received for a specific port, TCP or UDP places the incoming segments in the appropriate queue. For instance, if the application request is for HTTP, the TCP process running on a web server places incoming segments in the web server *queue*. These segments are then passed up to the HTTP application as quickly as HTTP can accept them.

Segments with port 25 specified are placed in a separate queue that is directed toward email services. In this manner, Transport Layer protocols enable servers at the ISP to host many different applications and services simultaneously.

Refer to
Figure
in online course

In any Internet transaction, there is a source host and a destination host, normally a client and a server. The TCP processes on the sending and receiving hosts are slightly different. Clients are active and request connections, while servers are passive, and listen for and accept connections.

Server processes are usually statically assigned well-known port numbers from 0 to 1023. Well-known port numbers enable a client application to assign the correct destination port when generating a request for services.

Clients also require port numbers to identify the requesting client application. Source ports are dynamically assigned from the port range 1024 to 65535. This port assignment acts like a return address for the requesting application. The Transport Layer protocols keep track of the source port and the application that initiated the request, so that when a response is returned, it can be forwarded to the correct application.

Refer to
Figure
in online course

The combination of the Transport Layer port number and the Network Layer IP address of the host uniquely identifies a particular application process running on an individual host device. This combination is called a *socket*. A socket pair, consisting of the source and destination IP addresses and port numbers, is also unique and identifies the specific conversation between the two hosts.

A client socket might look like this, with 7151 representing the source port number:

192.168.1.1:7151

The socket on a web server might be:

10.10.10.101:80

Together, these two sockets combine to form a socket pair:

192.168.1.1:7151, 10.10.10.101:80

With the creation of sockets, communication endpoints are known so that data can move from an application on one host to an application on another. Sockets enable multiple processes running on a client to distinguish themselves from each other, and multiple connections to a server process to be distinguished from each other.

7.3 Domain Name System

7.3.1 TCP/IP Host Name

Refer to
Figure
in online course

Communication between source and destination hosts over the Internet requires a valid IP address for each host. However, numeric IP addresses, especially the hundreds of thousands of addresses assigned to servers available over the Internet, are difficult for humans to remember. Human-readable domain names, like cisco.com, are easier for people to use. Network naming systems are designed to translate human-readable names into machine-readable IP addresses that can be used to communicate over the network.

Humans use network naming systems every day when surfing the web or sending email messages, and may not even realize it. Naming systems work as a hidden but integral part of network communication. For example, to browse to the Cisco Systems website, open a browser and enter http://www.cisco.com in the address field. The www.cisco.com is a network name that is associated with a specific IP address. Typing the server IP address into the browser brings up the same web page.

Network naming systems are a human convenience to help users reach the resource they need without having to remember the complex IP address.

Refer to
Figure
in online course

In the early days of the Internet, host names and IP addresses were managed through the use of a single HOSTS file located on a centrally administered server.

The central HOSTS file contained the mapping of the host name and IP address for every device connected to the early Internet. Each site could download the HOSTS file and use it to resolve host names on the network. When a host name was entered, the sending host would check the downloaded HOSTS file to obtain the IP address of the destination device.

At first, the HOSTS file was acceptable for the limited number of computer systems participating in the Internet. As the network grew, so did the number of hosts needing name-to-IP translations. It became impossible to keep the HOSTS file up to date. As a result, a new method to resolve host names to IP addresses was developed. DNS was created for domain name to address resolution. DNS uses a distributed set of servers to resolve the names associated with the numbered addresses. The single, centrally administered HOSTS file is no longer needed.

However, virtually all computer systems still maintain a local HOSTS file. A local HOSTS file is created when TCP/IP is loaded on a host device. As part of the name resolution process on a computer system, the HOSTS file is scanned even before the more robust DNS service is queried. A local HOSTS file can be used for troubleshooting or to override records found in a DNS server.

Refer to
Lab Activity
for this chapter

Lab Activity

Set up name resolution using the HOSTS file.

7.3.2 DNS Hierarchy

Refer to
Figure
in online course

DNS solves the shortcomings of the HOSTS file. The structure of DNS is hierarchical, with a distributed database of host name to IP mappings spread across many DNS servers all over the world. This is unlike a HOSTS file, which requires all mappings to be maintained on one server.

DNS uses domain names to form the hierarchy. The naming structure is broken down into small, manageable zones. Each DNS server maintains a specific database file and is only responsible for managing name-to-IP mappings for that small portion of the entire DNS structure. When a DNS server receives a request for a name translation that is not within its DNS zone, the DNS server forwards the request to another DNS server within the proper *zone* for translation.

DNS is scalable because host name resolution is spread across multiple servers.

Refer to
Figure
in online course

DNS is made up of three components.

Resource Records and Domain Namespace

A resource record is a data record in the database file of a DNS zone. It is used to identify a type of host, a host IP address, or a parameter of the DNS database.

The domain namespace refers to the hierarchical naming structure for organizing resource records. The domain namespace is made up of various domains, or groups, and the resource records within each group.

Domain Name System Servers

Domain name system servers maintain the databases that store resource records and information about the domain namespace structure. DNS servers attempt to resolve client queries using the domain namespace and resource records it maintains in its zone database files. If the name server does not have the requested information in its DNS zone database, it uses additional predefined name servers to help resolve the name-to-IP query.

Resolvers

Resolvers are applications or operating system functions that run on DNS clients and DNS servers. When a domain name is used, the resolver queries the DNS server to translate that name to an IP address. A resolver is loaded on a DNS client, and is used to create the DNS name query that is sent to a DNS server. Resolvers are also loaded on DNS servers. If the DNS server does not have the name-to-IP mapping requested, it uses the resolver to forward the request to another DNS server.

Refer to
Figure
in online course

DNS uses a hierarchical system to provide name resolution. The hierarchy looks like an inverted tree, with the root at the top and branches below.

At the top of the hierarchy, the root servers maintain records about how to reach the top-level domain servers, which in turn have records that point to the second-level domain servers.

The different top-level domains represent either the type of organization or the country of origin. Examples of top-level domains are:

.au - Australia

.co - Colombia

.com - a business or industry

.jp - Japan

.org - a nonprofit organization

Under top-level domains are *second-level domain* names, and below them are other lower level domains.

Refer to
Figure
in online course

The root DNS server may not know exactly where the host H1.cisco.com is located, but it does have a record for the .com top-level domain. Likewise, the servers within the .com domain may not have a record for H1.cisco.com either, but they do have a record for the cisco.com domain. The DNS servers within the cisco.com domain do have the record for H1.cisco.com and can resolve the address.

DNS relies on this hierarchy of decentralized servers to store and maintain these resource records. The resource records contain domain names that the server can resolve, and alternate servers that can also process requests.

The name H1.cisco.com is referred to as a fully qualified domain name (*FQDN*) or DNS name, because it defines the exact location of the computer within the hierarchical DNS namespace.

7.3.3 DNS Name Resolution

Refer to
Figure
in online course

When a host needs to resolve a DNS name, it uses the resolver to contact a DNS server within its domain. The resolver knows the IP address of the DNS server to contact because it is preconfigured as part of the host IP configuration.

When the DNS server receives the request from the client resolver, it first checks the local DNS records it has cached in its memory. If it is unable to resolve the IP address locally, the server uses its resolver to forward the request to another preconfigured DNS server. This process continues until the IP address is resolved. The name resolution information is sent back to the original DNS server, which uses the information to respond to the initial query.

During the process of resolving a DNS name, each DNS server caches, or stores, the information it receives as replies to the queries. The cached information enables the DNS server to reply more quickly to subsequent resolver requests, because the server first checks the cache records before querying other DNS servers.

DNS servers only cache information for a limited amount of time. DNS servers should not cache information for too long because host name records do periodically change. If a DNS server had old information cached, it may give out the wrong IP address for a computer.

Refer to
Lab Activity
for this chapter

Lab Activity

Examine the interface of a Windows DNS server to view the cached information from a DNS lookup.

Refer to
Figure
in online course

In the early implementations of DNS, resource records for hosts were all added and updated manually. However, as networks grew and the number of host records needing to be managed increased, it became very inefficient to maintain the resource records manually. Furthermore, when DHCP is used, the resource records within the DNS zone have to be updated even more frequently. To make updating the DNS zone information easier, the DNS protocol was changed to allow computer systems to update their own record in the DNS zone through dynamic updates.

Dynamic updates enable DNS client computers to register and dynamically update their resource records with a DNS server whenever changes occur. To use *dynamic update*, the DNS server and the DNS clients, or DHCP server, must support the dynamic update feature. Dynamic updates on the DNS server are not enabled by default, and must be explicitly enabled. Most current operating systems support the use of dynamic updates.

Refer to
Figure
in online course

DNS servers maintain the zone database for a given portion of the overall DNS hierarchy. Resource records are stored within that DNS zone.

DNS zones can be either a forward lookup or reverse lookup zone. They can also be either a primary or a secondary forward or reverse lookup zone. Each zone type has a specific role within the overall DNS infrastructure.

Forward Lookup Zones

A *forward lookup* zone is a standard DNS zone that resolves fully qualified domain names to IP addresses. This is the zone type that is most commonly found when surfing the Internet. When typing a website address, such as www.cisco.com, a recursive query is sent to the local DNS server to resolve that name to an IP address to connect to the remote web server.

Reverse Lookup Zones

A *reverse lookup* zone is a special zone type that resolves an IP address to a fully qualified domain name. Some applications use reverse lookups to identify computer systems that are actively communicating with them. There is an entire reverse lookup DNS hierarchy on the Internet that enables any publicly registered IP address to be resolved. Many private networks choose to implement their own local reverse lookup zones to help identify computer systems within their network. Reverse lookups on IP addresses can be found using the `ping -a` [ip_address] command.

Primary Zones

A primary DNS zone is a zone that can be modified. When a new resource record needs to be added or an existing record needs to be updated or deleted, the change is made on a primary DNS zone. When you have a primary zone on a DNS server, that server is said to be authoritative for that DNS zone, since it will have the answer for DNS queries for records within that zone. There can only be one primary DNS zone for any given DNS domain; however, you can have a primary forward and primary reverse lookup zone.

Secondary Zones

A secondary zone is a read-only backup zone maintained on a separate DNS server than the primary zone. The secondary zone is a copy of the primary zone and receives updates to the zone information from the primary server. Since the secondary zone is a read-only copy of the zone, all updates to the records need to be done on the corresponding primary zone. You can also have secondary zones for both forward and reverse lookup zones. Depending on the availability requirements for a DNS zone, you may have many secondary DNS zones spread across many DNS servers.

Refer to Lab Activity for this chapter

Lab Activity

Using a Windows server, create primary and secondary DNS zones.

7.3.4 Implementing DNS Solutions

Refer to Figure in online course

There is more than one way to implement DNS solutions.

ISP DNS Servers

ISPs typically maintain caching-only DNS servers. These servers are configured to forward all name resolution requests to the root servers on the Internet. Results are cached and used to reply to any future requests. Because ISPs typically have many customers, the number of cached DNS lookups is high. The large cache reduces network bandwidth by reducing the frequency that DNS queries that are forwarded to the root servers. Caching-only servers do not maintain any authoritative zone information, meaning that they do not store any name-to-IP mappings directly within their database.

Local DNS Servers

A business may run its own DNS server. The client computers on that network are configured to point to the local DNS server rather than the ISP DNS server. The local DNS server may maintain some authoritative entries for that zone, so it has name-to-IP mappings of any host within the zone. If the DNS server receives a request that it cannot resolve, it is forwarded. The cache required on a local server is relatively small compared to the ISP DNS server because of the smaller number of requests.

It is possible to configure local DNS servers to forward requests directly to the root DNS server. However, some administrators configure local DNS servers to forward all DNS requests to an upstream DNS server, such as the DNS server of the ISP. In this way, the local DNS server benefits from the large number of cached DNS entries of the ISP, rather than having to go through the entire lookup process starting from the root server.

Refer to
Figure
in online course

Losing access to DNS servers affects the visibility of public resources. If users type in a domain name that cannot be resolved, they cannot access the resource. For this reason, when an organization registers a domain name on the Internet, a minimum of two DNS servers must be provided with the registration. These servers are the ones that hold the DNS zone database. Redundant DNS servers ensure that if one fails, the other one is available for name resolution. This practice provides fault tolerance. If hardware resources permit, having more than two DNS servers within a zone provides additional protection and organization.

It is also a good idea to make sure that multiple DNS servers that host the zone information are located on different physical networks. For example, the primary DNS zone information can be stored on a DNS server on the local business premises. Usually the ISP hosts an additional secondary DNS server to ensure fault tolerance.

DNS is a critical network service. Therefore, DNS servers must be protected using firewalls and other security measures. If DNS fails, other web services are not accessible.

7.4 Services and Protocols

7.4.1 Services

Refer to
Figure
in online course

In addition to providing private and business customers with connectivity and DNS services, ISPs provide many business-oriented services to customers. These services are enabled by software installed on servers. Among the different services provided by ISPs are:

- email hosting
- website hosting
- e-commerce sites
- file storage and transfer
- message boards and blogs
- streaming video and audio services

TCP/IP Application Layer protocols enable many of these ISP services and applications. The most common TCP/IP Application Layer protocols are HTTP, FTP, SMTP, *POP3*, and *IMAP4*.

Some customers have greater concern about security, so these Application Layer protocols also include secure versions such as *FTPS* and *HTTPS*.

Refer to
Interactive Graphic
in online course.

Activity

Identify the protocols that are required for each server type.

Drag the protocol to the correct server type.

7.4.2 HTTP and HTTPS

Refer to **Figure** in online course

HTTP, one of the protocols in the TCP/IP suite, was originally developed to enable the retrieval of HTML-formatted web pages. It is now used for distributed, collaborative information sharing. HTTP has evolved through multiple versions. Most ISPs use HTTP version 1.1 to provide web-hosting services. Unlike earlier versions, version 1.1 enables a single web server to host multiple websites. It also permits persistent connections, so that multiple request and response messages can use the same connection, reducing the time it takes to initiate new TCP sessions.

HTTP specifies a request/response protocol. When a client, typically a web browser, sends a request message to a server, HTTP defines the message types that the client uses to request the web page. It also defines the message types that the server uses to respond.

Although it is remarkably flexible, HTTP is not a secure protocol. The request messages send information to the server in plain text that can be intercepted and read. Similarly, the server responses, typically HTML pages, are also sent unencrypted.

For secure communication across the Internet, Secure HTTP (HTTPS) is used for accessing or posting web server information. HTTPS can use authentication and encryption to secure data as it travels between the client and server. HTTPS specifies additional rules for passing data between the Application Layer and the Transport Layer.

Refer to **Figure** in online course

When contacting an HTTP server to download a web page, a uniform resource locator (URL) is used to locate the server and a specific resource. The URL identifies:

- Protocol being used
- Domain name of the server being accessed
- Location of the resource on the server, such as http://example.com/example1/index.htm

Many web server applications allow short URLs. Short URLs are popular because they are easier to write down, remember, or share. With a short URL, a default resource page is assumed when a specific URL is typed. When a user types in a shortened URL, like http://example.com, the default page that is sent to the user is actually the http://example.com/example1/index.htm web page.

Refer to **Figure** in online course

HTTP supports *proxy services*. A proxy server allows clients to make indirect network connections to other network services. A proxy is a device in the communications stream that acts as a server to the client and as a client to a server.

The client connects to the proxy server and requests from the proxy a resource on a different server. The proxy connects to the specified server and retrieves the requested resource. It then forwards the resource back to the client.

The proxy server can cache the resulting page or resource for a configurable amount of time. Caching enables future clients to access the web page quickly, without having to access the actual server where the page is stored. Proxies are used for three reasons:

- Speed - Caching allows resources requested by one user to be available to subsequent users, without having to access the actual server where the page is stored.
- Security - Proxy servers can be used to intercept *computer virus*es and other malicious content and prevent them from being forwarded onto clients.
- Filtering - Proxy servers can view incoming HTTP messages and filter unsuitable and offensive web content.

Refer to
Figure
in online course

HTTP sends clear text messages back and forth between a client and a server. These text messages can be easily intercepted and read by unauthorized users. To safeguard data, especially confidential information, some ISPs provide secure web services by using HTTPS. HTTPS is HTTP over secure socket layer (SSL). HTTPS uses the same client request-server response process as HTTP, but the data stream is encrypted with SSL before being transported across the network.

When the HTTP data stream arrives at the server, the TCP layer passes it up to SSL in the Application Layer of the server, where it is decrypted.

The maximum number of simultaneous connections that a server can support for HTTPS is less than that for HTTP. HTTPS creates additional load and processing time on the server due to the encryption and decryption of traffic. To keep server performance up, HTTPS should only be used when necessary, such as when exchanging confidential information.

Refer to
Interactive Graphic
in online course.

Activity

Identify the characteristics of HTTP and HTTPS.

Drag the characteristics to the correct protocol.

7.4.3 FTP

Refer to
Figure
in online course

FTP is a connection-oriented protocol that uses TCP to communicate between a client FTP process and an FTP process on a server. FTP implementations include the functions of a protocol interpreter (*PI*) and a data transfer process (*DTP*). PI and DTP define two separate processes that work together to transfer files. As a result, FTP requires two connections to exist between the client and server, one to send control information and commands, and a second one for the actual file data transfer.

Protocol Interpreter (PI)

The PI function is the main control connection between the FTP client and the FTP server. It establishes the TCP connection and passes control information to the server. Control information includes commands to navigate through a file hierarchy and renaming or moving files. The control connection, or control stream, stays open until closed by the user. When a user wants to connect to an FTP server there are five basic steps:

Step 1. The user PI sends a connection request to the server PI on well-known port 21.

Step 2. The server PI replies and the connection is established.

Step 3. With the TCP control connection open, the server PI process begins the login sequence.

Step 4. The user enters credentials through the user interface and completes authentication.

Step 5. The data transfer process begins.

Data Transfer Process

DTP is a separate data transfer function. This function is enabled only when the user wants to actually transfer files to or from the FTP server. Unlike the PI connection, which remains open, the DTP connection closes automatically when the file transfer is complete.

Refer to
Figure
in online course

The two types of data transfer connections supported by FTP are active data connections and passive data connections.

Active Data Connections

In an active data connection, a client initiates a request to the server and opens a port for the expected data. The server then connects to the client on that port and the file transfer begins.

Passive Data Connections

In a passive data connection, the FTP server opens a random source port (greater than 1023). The server forwards its IP address and the random port number to the FTP client over the control stream. The server then waits for a connection from the FTP client to begin the data file transfer.

ISPs typically support passive data connections to their FTP servers. Firewalls often do not permit active FTP connections to hosts located on the inside network.

7.4.4 SMTP, POP3, and IMAP4

Refer to
Figure
in online course

One of the primary services offered by an ISP is email hosting. Email is a store-and-forward method of sending, storing, and retrieving electronic messages across a network. Email messages are stored in databases on mail servers. ISPs often maintain mail servers that support many different customer accounts.

Email clients communicate with mail servers to send and receive email. Mail servers communicate with other mail servers to transport messages from one domain to another. An email client does not communicate directly with another email client when sending email. Instead, both clients rely on the mail server to transport messages. This is true even when both users are in the same domain.

Email clients send messages to the email server configured in the application settings. When the server receives the message, it checks to see if the recipient domain is located on its local database. If it is not, it sends a DNS request to determine the mail server for the destination domain. When the IP address of the destination mail server is known, the email is sent to the appropriate server.

Email supports three separate protocols for operation: SMTP, POP3, and IMAP4. The Application Layer process that sends mail, either from a client to a server or between servers, implements SMTP. A client retrieves email using one of two Application Layer protocols: POP3 or IMAP4.

Refer to
Figure
in online course

SMTP transfers mail reliably and efficiently. For SMTP applications to work properly, the mail message must be formatted properly and SMTP processes must be running on both the client and server.

SMTP message formats require a message header and a message body. While the message body can contain any amount of text, the message header must have a properly formatted recipient email address and a sender address. Any other header information is optional.

When a client sends email, the client SMTP process connects with a server SMTP process on well-known port 25. After the connection is made, the client attempts to send mail to the server across the connection. When the server receives the message, it either places the message in a local account or forwards the message using the same SMTP connection process to another mail server.

The destination email server may not be online or may be busy when email messages are sent. Therefore, SMTP spools messages to be sent at a later time. Periodically, the server checks the queue for messages and attempts to send them again. If the message is still not delivered after a predetermined expiration time, it is returned to the sender as undeliverable.

Refer to
Figure
in online course

One of the required fields in an email message header is the recipient email address. The structure of an email address includes the email account name or an alias, in addition to the domain name of the mail server. An example of an email address:

recipient@cisco.com.

The @ symbol separates the account and the domain name of the server. When a DNS server receives a query for a name with an @ symbol, that indicates to the DNS server that it is looking up an IP address for a mail server.

When a message is sent to recipient@cisco.com, the domain name is sent to the DNS server to obtain the IP address of the domain mail server. Mail servers are identified in DNS by an MX record indicator. MX is a type of resource record stored on the DNS server. When the destination mail server receives the message, it stores the message in the appropriate mailbox. The mailbox location is determined based on the account specified in the first part of the email address, in this case, the recipient account. The message remains in the mailbox until the recipient connects to the server to retrieve the email.

If the mail server receives an email message that references an account that does not exist, the email is returned to the sender as undeliverable.

Refer to
Figure
in online course

Post Office Protocol - Version 3 (POP3) enables a workstation to retrieve mail from a mail server. With POP3, mail is downloaded from the server to the client and then deleted on the server.

The server starts the POP3 service by passively listening on TCP port 110 for client connection requests. When a client wants to make use of the service, it sends a request to establish a TCP connection with the server. When the connection is established, the POP3 server sends a greeting. The client and POP3 server then exchange commands and responses until the connection is closed or aborted.

Because email messages are downloaded to the client and removed from the server, there is not a centralized location where email messages are kept. Because POP3 does not store messages, it is undesirable for a small business that needs a centralized backup solution.

POP3 is desirable for an ISP, because it alleviates their responsibility for managing large amounts of storage for their email servers.

Refer to
Figure
in online course

Internet Message Access Protocol (IMAP4) is another protocol that describes a method to retrieve email messages. However, unlike POP3, when the user connects to an IMAP-capable server, copies of the messages are downloaded to the client application. The original messages are kept on the server until manually deleted. Users view copies of the messages in their email client software.

Users can create a file hierarchy on the server to organize and store mail. That file structure is duplicated on the email client as well. When a user decides to delete a message, the server synchronizes that action and deletes the message from the server.

For small- to medium-sized businesses, there are many advantages to using IMAP. IMAP can provide long-term storage of email messages on mail servers and allows for centralized backup. It also enables employees to access email messages from multiple locations, using different devices or client software. The mailbox folder structure that a user expects to see is available for viewing regardless of how the user accesses the mailbox.

For an ISP, IMAP may not be the protocol of choice. It can be expensive to purchase and maintain the disk space to support the large number of stored emails. Additionally, if customers expect their mailboxes to be backed up routinely, that can further increase the costs to the ISP.

Chapter Summary

Click through the buttons for summary information.

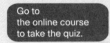

Chapter Quiz

Take the chapter quiz to check your knowledge.

Your Chapter Notes

CHAPTER 8

ISP Responsibility

Introduction

Refer to
Figure
in online course

8.1 ISP Security Considerations

8.1.1 ISP Security Services

Refer to
Figure
in online course

Any active Internet connection for a computer can make that computer a target for malicious activity. *Malware*, or malicious software such as a computer virus, *worm*, or *spyware*, can arrive in an email or be downloaded from a website. Problems that cause large-scale failures in ISP networks often originate from unsecured desktop systems at the ISP customer locations.

If the ISP is hosting any web or e-commerce sites, the ISP may have confidential files with financial data or bank account information stored on their servers. The ISP is required to maintain the customer data in a secure way.

ISPs play a big role in helping to protect the home and business users that use their services. The security services that they provide also protect the servers that are located at the service provider premise. Service providers are often called upon to help their customers secure their local networks and workstations to reduce the risks of compromise.

There are many actions that can be taken both at the local site and the ISP to secure operating systems, data stored on operating systems, and data transmitted between computer systems.

Refer to
Figure
in online course

If an ISP is providing web hosting or email services for a customer, it is important that the ISP protect that information from malicious attack. This protection can be complicated because ISPs often use a single server, or cluster of servers, to maintain data that belongs to more than one customer.

To help prevent attacks on these vulnerabilities, many ISPs provide managed desktop security services for their customers. An important part of the job of an on-site support technician is to implement security best practices on client computers. Some of the security services that an ISP support technician can provide include:

- Helping clients to create secure passwords for devices
- Securing applications using patch management and software upgrades
- Removing unnecessary applications and services that can create vulnerabilities
- Ensuring applications and services are available to the users that need them and no one else
- Configuring desktop firewalls and virus-checking software

- Performing security scans on software and services to determine vulnerabilities

that the technician must protect from attack

8.1.2 Security Practices

Refer to
Figure
in online course

It is critical that ISPs have measures in place to protect the information of its customers from malicious attack. Common data security features and procedures include:

- Encrypting data stored on server hard drives

- Using permissions to secure access to files and folders

- Permit or deny access based on the user account or group membership

- Assign different levels of access permission based on the user account or group membership

When assigning permissions to files and folders, a security best practice is to apply permissions based on the "principle of least privilege". This means giving users access to only those resources that are required for them to be able do their job. It also means giving the appropriate level of permission, for example read-only access or write access.

Refer to
Figure
in online course

Authentication, *Authorization*, and *Accounting* (*AAA*) is a three-step process used by network administrators to make it difficult for attackers to gain access to a network.

Authentication requires users to prove their identity using a username and password. Authentication databases are typically stored on servers that use the RADIUS or TACACS protocols.

Authorization gives users rights to access specific resources and perform specific tasks.

Accounting tracks which applications are used and the length of time that they are used.

For example, authentication acknowledges that a user named "student" exists and is able to log on. Authorization services specify that user student can access host server XYZ using Telnet. Accounting tracks that user student accessed host server XYZ using Telnet on a specific day for 15 minutes.

AAA can be used on various types of network connections. AAA requires a database to keep track of user credentials, permissions, and account statistics. Local authentication is the simplest form of AAA and keeps a local database on the gateway router. If an organization has more than a handful of users authenticating with AAA, the organization must use a database on a separate server.

8.1.3 Data Encryption

Refer to
Figure
in online course

ISPs must also be concerned with securing data that is transmitted to and from their servers. By default, data sent over the network is unsecured and transmitted in clear text. Unauthorized individuals can intercept unsecured data as it is being transmitted. Capturing data in transit bypasses all file system security that is set on the data. There are methods available to protect against this security issue.

Encryption

Digital encryption is the process of encrypting all transmitted data between the client and the server. Many of the protocols used to transmit data offer a secure version that uses digital encryption. As a best practice, use the secure version of a protocol whenever the data being exchanged between two computers is confidential.

For example, if a user must submit a username and password to log on to an e-commerce website, a secure protocol is required to protect the username and password information from being captured. Secure protocols are also needed any time a user must submit a credit card or bank account information.

When surfing the Internet and viewing publicly accessible websites, securing the transmitted data is not necessary. Using a secure protocol in this situation can lead to additional computational overhead and slower response time.

Refer to
Figure
in online course

There are many network protocols used by applications. Some offer secure versions and some do not:

- *Web servers* - Web servers use HTTP by default, which is not a secure protocol. Using HTTPS, which uses the secure socket layer (SSL) protocol, enables the exchange of data to be performed securely.

- *Email servers* - Email servers use several different protocols, including SMTP, POP3, and IMAP4. When a user logs on to an email server, POP3 and IMAP4 require a username and password for authentication. By default, this information is sent without security and can be captured. POP3 can be secured by using SSL. SMTP and IMAP4 can use either SSL or Transport Layer Security (*TLS*) as a security protocol.

- *Telnet servers* - Using Telnet to remotely log into a Cisco router or switch creates an unsecure connection. Telnet sends authentication information and any commands a user types across the network in clear text. Use the Secure Shell (SSH) protocol to authenticate and work with the router or switch securely.

- *FTP servers* - FTP is also an unsecure protocol. When logging into an FTP server, authentication information is sent in clear text. FTP can use SSL to securely exchange authentication and data. Some versions of FTP can also use SSH.

- *File servers* - File servers can use many different protocols to exchange data, depending on the computer operating system. In most cases, file server protocols do not offer a secure version.

IP Security (*IPSec*) is another Network Layer security protocol that can be used to secure any Application Layer protocol used for communication. This includes file server protocols that do not offer any other security protocol version.

Refer to
Lab Activity
for this chapter

Lab Activity

Perform the data security tasks needed to analyze and secure local and transmitted data.

8.2 Security Tools

8.2.1 Access Control Lists and Port Filtering

Refer to
Figure
in online course

Even with the use of AAA and encryption, there are still many different types of attacks that an ISP must protect against. ISPs are especially vulnerable to denial-of-service (*DoS*) attacks, because the ISP may host sites for many different registered domain names that may or may not require authentication. Currently, there are three key types of DoS attacks.

DoS

A standard DoS attack is when a server or service is attacked to prevent legitimate access to that service. Some examples of standard DoS attacks are *SYN floods*, ping floods, *LAND attacks*, bandwidth consumption attacks, and *buffer overflow attacks*.

DDoS

A distributed denial-of-service (*DDoS*) attack occurs when multiple computers are used to attack a specific target. The attacker has access to many compromised computer systems, usually on the Internet. Because of this, the attacker can remotely launch the attack. DDoS attacks are usually the same kinds of attacks as standard DoS attacks, except that DDoS attacks are run from many computer systems simultaneously.

DRDoS

A distributed reflected denial-of-service (DRDoS) attack occurs when an attacker sends a spoofed, or mock, request to many computer systems on the Internet, with the source address modified to be the targeted computer system. The computer systems that receive the request respond. When the computer systems respond to the request, all the requests are directed at the target computer system. Because the attack is reflected, it is very difficult to determine the originator of the attack.

Refer to
Figure
in online course

ISPs must be able to filter out network traffic, such as DoS attacks, that can be harmful to the operation of their network or servers. *Port filter*ing and access control lists (*ACL*) can be used to control traffic to servers and networking equipment.

Port Filtering

Port filtering controls the flow of traffic based on a specific TCP or UDP port. Many server operating systems have options to restrict access using port filtering. Port filtering is also used by network routers and switches to help control traffic flow and to secure access to the device.

Access Control Lists

ACLs define traffic that is permitted or denied through the network based on the source and destination IP addresses. ACLs can also permit or deny traffic based on the source and destination ports of the protocol being used. Additonally, ICMP and routing update traffic can be controlled using ACLs. Administrators create ACLs on network devices, such as routers, to control whether or not traffic is forwarded or blocked.

ACLs are only the first line of defense and are not enough to secure a network. ACLs only prevent access to a network; they do not protect the network from all types of malicious attacks.

Refer to
Lab Activity
for this chapter

Lab Activity

Determine where to implement ACLs and port filters to help protect the network.

8.2.2 Firewalls

Refer to
Figure
in online course

A firewall is network hardware or software that defines which traffic can come into and go out of sections of the network and how traffic is handled.

ACLs are one of the tools used by firewalls. ACLs control which type of traffic is allowed to pass through the firewall. The direction the traffic is allowed to travel can also be controlled. In a medium-sized network, the amount of traffic and networking protocols needing to be controlled is quite large, and firewall ACLs can become very complicated.

Firewalls use ACLs to control which traffic is passed or blocked. They are constantly evolving as new capabilities are developed and new threats are discovered.

Different firewalls offer different types of features. For example, a dynamic packet filter firewall or stateful firewall keeps track of the actual communication process occurring between the source and destination devices. It does this by using a state table. When a communication stream is approved, only traffic that belongs to one of these communication streams is permitted through the firewall. The Cisco IOS Firewall software is embedded in the Cisco IOS software and allows the user to turn a router into a network layer firewall with dynamic or stateful inspection.

Firewalls are constantly evolving as new capabilities are developed and new threats are discovered. The more functionality embedded in a firewall, the more time it takes for packets to be processed.

Refer to
Figure
in online course

Firewalls can provide perimeter security for the entire network and for internal local network segments, such as server farms.

Within an ISP network or a medium-sized business, firewalls are typically implemented in multiple layers. Traffic that comes in from an untrusted network first encounters a packet filter on the border router. Permitted traffic goes through the border router to an internal firewall to route traffic to a demilitarized zone (*DMZ*). A DMZ is used to store servers that users from the Internet are allowed to access. Only traffic that is permitted access to these servers is permitted into the DMZ. Firewalls also control what kind of traffic is permitted into the protected, local network itself. The traffic that is allowed into the internal network is usually traffic that is being sent due to a specific request by an internal device. For example, if an internal device requests a web page from an external server, the firewall permits the requested web page to enter the internal network.

Some organizations can choose to implement internal firewalls to protect sensitive areas. Internal firewalls are used to restrict access to areas of the network that need to have additional protection. Internal firewalls separate and protect business resources on servers from users inside the organization. Internal firewalls prevent external and internal hackers, as well as unintentional internal attacks and malware.

Refer to **Packet
Tracer Activity**
for this chapter

Packet Tracer Activity

In this activity, you are a technician who provides network support for a medium-sized business. The business has grown and includes a research and development department working on a new, very confidential project. The livelihood of the project depends on protecting the data used by the research and development team. Your job is to install firewalls to help protect the network, based on specific requirements.

8.2.3 IDS and IPS

Refer to
Figure
in online course

ISPs also have a responsibility to prevent, when possible, intrusions into their networks and the networks of customers who purchase managed services. There are two tools often utilized by ISPs to accomplish this.

Intrusion Detection System (IDS)

An *IDS* is a software- or hardware-based solution that passively listens to network traffic. Network traffic does not pass through an IDS device. Instead, the IDS device monitors traffic through a network interface. When the IDS detects malicious traffic, it sends an alert to a preconfigured management station.

Intrusion Prevention System (IPS)

An *IPS* is an active physical device or software feature. Traffic travels in one interface of the IPS and out the other. The IPS examines the actual data packets that are in the network traffic and works in real time to permit or deny packets that want access into the network

IDS and IPS technologies are deployed as sensors. An IDS or an IPS sensor can be any of the following:

- Router configured with Cisco IOS version IPS

- Appliance (hardware) specifically designed to provide dedicated IDS or IPS services

- Network module installed in an adaptive security appliance (ASA), switch, or router

IDS and IPS sensors respond differently to incidences detected on the network, but both have roles within a network.

Refer to
Figure
in online course

IDS solutions are reactive when it comes to detecting intrusions. They detect intrusions based on a *signature* for network traffic or computer activity. They do not stop the initial traffic from passing through to the destination, but react to the detected activity.

When properly configured, the IDS can block further malicious traffic by actively reconfiguring network devices, such as security appliances or routers, in response to malicious traffic detection. It is important to realize that the original malicious traffic has already passed through the network to the intended destination and cannot be blocked. Only subsequent traffic is blocked. In this regard, IDS devices cannot prevent some intrusions from being successful.

IDS solutions are often used on the untrusted perimeter of a network, outside of the firewall. Here the IDS can analyze the type of traffic that is hitting the firewall and determine how attacks are executed. The firewall can be used to block most malicious traffic. An IDS can also be placed inside the firewall to detect firewall misconfigurations. When the IDS sensor is placed here, any alarms that go off indicate that malicious traffic has been allowed through the firewall. These alarms mean that the firewall has not been configured correctly.

Refer to
Figure
in online course

IPS

Unlike IDS solutions, which are reactive, IPS solutions are proactive. They block all suspicious activity in real time. An IPS is able to examine almost the entire data packet from Layer 2 to Layer 7 of the OSI model. When the IPS detects malicious traffic, it blocks the malicious traffic immediately. The IPS then sends an alert to a management station about the intrusion. The original and subsequent malicious traffic is blocked as the IPS proactively prevents attacks.

An IPS is an intrusion detection appliance, not software. The IPS is most often placed inside the firewall. This is because it can examine most of the data packet and, therefore, be used to protect server applications if malicious traffic is being sent. The firewall typically does not examine the entire data packet, whereas the IPS does. The firewall drops most of the packets that are not allowed, but may still allow some malicious packets through. The IPS has a smaller number of packets to examine, so it can examine the entire packet. This allows the IPS to immediately stop new attacks that the firewall was not originally configured to deny. IPS can also stop attacks that the firewall is unable to deny based on limitations of the firewall.

Refer to
Interactive Graphic
in online course.

Activity

Determine how to protect the network from intrusions using IPS and IDS network equipment.

Click each statement that applies.

8.2.4 Wireless Security

Refer to
Figure
in online course

Some ISPs offer services to create wireless hot spots for customers to log on to wireless local-area networks (*WLANs*). A wireless network is easy to implement, but is vulnerable when not properly configured. Because the wireless signal travels through walls, it can be accessed outside the business premises. A wireless network can be secured by changing the default settings, enabling authentication, or enabling MAC address filtering.

Changing Default Settings

The default values for the SSID, usernames, and passwords on a wireless access point should be changed. Additionally, broadcasting of the SSID should be disabled.

Enabling Authentication

Authentication is the process of permitting entry to a network based on a set of credentials. It is used to verify that the device attempting to connect to the network is trusted. There are three types of authentication methods that can be used:

- *Open authentication* - Any and all clients are able to have access regardless of who they are. Open authentication is most often used on public wireless networks.

- *Pre-shared key (PSK)* - Requires a matching, preconfigured key on both the server and the client. When connecting, the access point sends a random string of bytes to the client. The client accepts the string, encrypts it (or scrambles it) based on the key, and sends it back to the access point. The access point gets the encrypted string and uses its key to decrypt (or unscramble) it. If they match, authentication is successful.

- *Extensible Authentication Protocol (EAP)* - Provides mutual, or two-way, authentication and user authentication. When EAP software is installed on the client, the client communicates with a backend authentication server, such as RADIUS.

Enabling MAC Address Filtering

MAC address filtering prevents unwanted computers from connecting to a network by restricting MAC addresses. It is possible, however, to clone a MAC address. Therefore, other security measures should be implemented along with MAC address filtering.

Refer to **Figure** in online course

It is important to set encryption on transmitted packets sent across a wireless network. There are three major encryption types for wireless networks:

- *WEP -* Wired Equivalent Privacy (*WEP*) provides data security by encrypting data that is sent between wireless nodes. WEP uses a 64, 128, or 256 bit pre-shared hexadecimal key to encrypt the data. A major weakness of WEP is its use of static encryption keys. The same key is used by every device to encrypt every packet transmitted. There are many WEP cracking tools available on the Internet. WEP should be used only with older equipment that does not support newer wireless security protocols.

- *WPA -* Wifi Protected Access (*WPA*) is a newer wireless encryption protocol that uses an improved encryption algorithm called Temporal Key Integrity Protocol (*TKIP*). TKIP generates a unique key for each client and rotates the security keys at a configurable interval. WPA provides a mechanism for mutual authentication. Because both the client and the access point have the key, it is never transmitted.

- *WPA2 -* WPA2 is a new, improved version of WPA. WPA2 uses the more secure Advanced Encryption Standard (*AES*) technology.

Refer to **Packet Tracer Activity** for this chapter

Packet Tracer Activity

In this activity, you will configure WEP security on both a Linksys wireless router and a workstation.

*Note: WPA is not supported by Packet tracer at this time. However, WEP and WPA are enabled by a similar process.

8.2.5 Host Security

Refer to **Figure** in online course

Regardless of the layers of defense that exist on the network, all servers are still susceptible to attack if they are not properly secured. ISP servers are especially vulnerable because they are generally accessible from the Internet. New vulnerabilities for servers are discovered every day, so it is critical for an ISP to protect its servers from known and unknown vulnerabilities whenever possible. One way they accomplish this is by using host-based firewalls.

A host-based firewall is software that runs directly on a host operating system. It protects the host from malicious attacks that might have made it through all other layers of defense. Host-based firewalls control inbound and outbound network traffic. These firewalls allow filtering based on a computer address and port, therefore offering additional protection over regular port filtering.

Host-based firewalls typically come with predefined rules that block all incoming network traffic. Exceptions are added to the firewall rule set to permit the correct mixture of inbound and outbound network traffic. When enabling host-based firewalls, it is important to balance the need to allow the network resources required to complete job tasks, with the need to prevent applications from being left vulnerable to malicious attacks. Many server operating systems are preconfigured with a simple host-based firewall with limited options. More advanced third-party packages are also available.

ISPs use host-based firewalls to restrict access to the specific services a server offers. By using a host-based firewall, the ISP protects their servers and the data of their customers by blocking access to the extraneous ports that are available.

Refer to **Figure** in online course

ISP servers that utilize host-based firewalls are protected from a variety of different types of attacks and vulnerabilities.

Known Attacks

Host-based firewalls recognize malicious activity based on updatable signatures or patterns. They detect a known attack and block traffic on the port used by the attack.

Exploitable Services

Host-based firewalls protect exploitable services running on servers by preventing access to the ports that the service is using. Some host-based firewalls can also inspect the contents of a packet to see if it contains malicious code. Web and email servers are common targets for service exploits, and can be protected if the host-based firewall is capable of performing packet inspection.

Worms and Viruses

Worms and viruses propagate by exploiting vulnerabilities in services and other weaknesses in operating systems. Host-based firewalls prevent this malware from gaining access to servers. They can also help prevent the spread of worms and viruses by controlling outbound traffic originating from a server.

Back Doors and Trojans

Back doors and *Trojan Horses* allow hackers to remotely gain access to servers on a network. The software typically works by sending a message to let the hacker know of a successful infection. It then provides a service that the hacker can use to gain access to the system. Host-based firewalls can prevent a Trojan from sending a message by limiting outbound network access. It can also prevent the attacker from connecting to any services.

Refer to **Figure** in online course

In addition to host-based firewalls, anti-X software can be installed as a more comprehensive security measure. Anti-X software protects computer systems from viruses, worms, spyware, malware, *phishing*, and even *spam*. Many ISPs offer customers anti-X software as part of their comprehensive security services. Not all anti-X software protects against the same threats. The ISP should constantly review which threats the anti-X software actually protects against and make recommendations based on a threat analysis of the company.

Many anti-X software packages allow for remote management. This includes a notification system that can alert the administrator or support technician about an infection via email or pager. Immediate notification to the proper individual can drastically reduce the impact of the infection. Using anti-X software does not diminish the number of threats to the network but reduces the risk of being infected.

Occasionally infections and attacks still occur and can be very destructive. It is important to have an incident management process to track all incidences and the corresponding resolutions to help prevent the infection from reoccurring. Incident management is required by ISPs that manage and maintain customer data, because the ISP has committed to the protection and the integrity of the data they host for their customers. For example, if the ISP network was the target of a hacker and, as a result, thousands of credit card numbers that were stored in a database that the ISP manages were stolen, the customer would need to be notified so that they could notify the card holders.

Lab Activity

Recommend an anti-X software package for a small business.

8.3 Monitoring and Managing the ISP

8.3.1 Service Level Agreements

An ISP and a user usually have a contract known as a service level agreement (SLA). It documents the expectations and obligations of both parties. An SLA typically includes the following parts:

- Service description
- Costs
- Tracking and reporting
- Problem management
- Security
- Termination
- Penalties for service outages
- Availability, performance, and reliability

The SLA is an important document that clearly outlines the management, monitoring, and maintenance of a network.

Lab Activity

Examine an SLA and practice interpreting the sections of the SLA.

8.3.2 Monitoring Network Link Performance

The ISP is responsible for monitoring and checking device connectivity. This responsibility includes any equipment that belongs to the ISP and equipment at the customer end that the ISP agreed to monitor in the SLA. Monitoring and configuration can be performed either out-of-band with a direct console connection, or in-band using a network connection.

Out-of-band management is useful in initial configurations if the device is not accessible via the network, or if a visual inspection of the device is necessary.

Most ISPs are not able to visually inspect or have physical access to all devices. An in-band management tool allows for easier administration because the technician does not require a physical connection. For this reason, in-band management is preferred over out-of-band management for managing servers and networking devices that are accessible on the network. Additionally, conventional in-band tools can provide more management functionality than may be possible with out-of-band management, such as an overall view of the network design. Traditional in-band management protocols include Telnet, SSH, HTTP, and Simple Network Management Protocol (SNMP).

There are many embedded tools, commercial tools, and shareware tools available that use these management protocols. For example, HTTP access is through a web browser. Some applications, such as Cisco SDM, use this access for in-band management.

Refer to
Lab Activity
for this chapter

Lab Activity

Download, install, and then conduct a network capture with Wireshark.

8.3.3 Device Management Using In-band Tools

Refer to
Figure
in online course

After a new network device is installed at the customer premise, it must be monitored from the remote ISP location. There are times that minor configuration changes need to be made without the physical presence of a technician at the customer site.

A Telnet client can be used over an IP network connection to connect to a device in-band for the purpose of monitoring and administering it. A connection using Telnet is called a Virtual Terminal (VTY) session or connection. Telnet is a client/server protocol. The connecting device runs the Telnet client. To support Telnet client connections, the connected device, or server, runs a service called a Telnet daemon.

Most operating systems include an Application Layer Telnet client. On a Microsoft Windows PC, Telnet can be run from the command prompt. Other common terminal emulation applications that run as Telnet clients are HyperTerminal, Minicom, and TeraTerm. Devices such as routers run both the Telnet client and the Telnet daemon, and can act as either the client or server.

After a Telnet connection is established, users can perform any authorized function on the server, just as if they were using a command line session on the server itself. If authorized, users can start and stop processes, configure the device, and even shut down the system.

A Telnet session can be initiated using the router CLI with the `telnet` command followed by the IP address or domain name. A Telnet client can connect to multiple servers simultaneously. On a Cisco router, the keystroke sequence Ctrl-Shift-6 X to toggles between Telnet sessions. Additionally, a Telnet server can support multiple client connections. On a router acting as a server, the `show sessions` command displays all client connections.

Refer to
Lab Activity
for this chapter

Lab Activity

Use Telnet to manage remote network devices.

Refer to
Figure
in online course

While the Telnet protocol supports user authentication, it does not support the transport of encrypted data. All data exchanged during a Telnet session is transported as plain text across the network. This means that the data can be intercepted and easily understood, including the username and password used to authenticate the device.

If security is a concern, the Secure Shell (SSH) protocol offers an alternate and secure method for server access. SSH provides secure remote login and other network services. It also provides stronger authentication than Telnet and supports the transport of session data using encryption. As a best practice, network professionals should always use SSH in place of Telnet whenever possible.

There are two versions of the SSH server service. Which SSH version is supported depends on the Cisco IOS image loaded on the device. There are many different SSH client software packages available for PCs. An SSH client must support the SSH version configured on the server.

Refer to
Lab Activity
for this chapter

Lab Activity

Configure a remote router using SSH.

8.3.4 Using SNMP and Syslog

Refer to
Figure
in online course

SNMP is a network management protocol that enables administrators to gather data about the network and corresponding devices. SNMP management system software is available in tools such as *CiscoWorks*. There are free versions of CiscoWorks available for download on the Internet. SNMP management agent software is often embedded in operating systems on servers, routers, and switches.

SNMP is made up of four main components:

- *Management station* - Computer with the SNMP management application loaded that is used by the administrator to monitor and configure the network.

- *Management agent* - Software installed on a device managed by SNMP.

- *Management Information Base (MIB)* - Database that a device keeps about itself concerning network performance parameters.

- *Network management protocol* - Communication protocol used between the management station and the management agent.

Refer to
Figure
in online course

The management station contains the SNMP management applications that the administrator uses to configure devices on the network. It also stores data about those devices. The management station collects information by polling the devices. A poll occurs when the management station requests specific information from an agent.

The agent reports to the management station by responding to the polls. When the management station polls an agent, the agent calls on statistics that have accumulated in the MIB.

Agents can also be configured with traps. A *trap* is an alarm-triggering event. Certain areas of the agent are configured with thresholds, or maximums, that must be maintained, such as the amount of traffic that can access a specific port. If the threshold is exceeded, the agent sends an alert message to the management station. Traps free the management station from continuously polling network devices.

Management stations and managed devices are identified by a community ID, called a community string. The community string on the SMNP agent must match the community string on the SMNP management station. When an agent is required to send information to a management station due to a poll or trap event, it will first verify the management station using the community string.

Refer to
Figure
in online course

Storing *device log*s and reviewing them periodically is an important part of network monitoring. *Syslog* is the standard for logging system events. Like SNMP, syslog is an Application Layer protocol that enables devices to send information to a *syslog daemon* that is installed and running on a management station.

A syslog system is composed of syslog servers and syslog clients. These servers accept and process log messages from syslog clients. A syslog client is a monitored device that generates and forwards log messages to syslog servers.

Log messages normally consist of a ID, type of message, a time stamp (date, time), which device has sent the message, and the message text. Depending on which network equipment is sending the syslog messages, it can contain more items than those listed.

8.4 Backups and Disaster Recovery

8.4.1 Backup Media

Refer to **Figure** in online course

Network management and monitoring software helps ISPs and businesses identify and correct network issues. This software can also help to correct the causes of network failures, such as those caused by malware and malicious activity, network functionality, and failed devices.

Regardless of the cause of failure, an ISP that hosts websites or email for customers must protect the web and email content from being lost. Losing the data stored on a website could mean hundreds, or even thousands, of hours recreating the content, not to mention the lost business that results from the downtime while the content is being restored.

Losing email messages that were stored on the ISP email server could potentially be devastating for a business that relies on the data within the emails. Some businesses are legally required to maintain records of all email correspondence, so losing email data is not acceptable.

Data backup is essential. The job of an IT professional is to reduce the risks of data loss and provide mechanisms for quick recovery of any data that is lost.

Refer to **Figure** in online course

When an ISP needs to back up its data, the cost of a backup solution and its effectiveness must be balanced. The choice of backup media can be complex because there are many factors that affect the choice.

Some of the factors include:

- Amount of data

- Cost of media

- Performance of media

- Reliability of media

- Ease of offsite storage

There are many types of backup media available, including tapes, optical discs, hard disks, and solid state devices.

Refer to **Figure** in online course

Tape remains one of the most common types of backup media available. Tapes have large capacities and remain the most cost-effective media on the market. For data volumes in excess of a single tape, autoloaders and libraries can swap tapes during the backup procedure, allowing the data to be stored on as many tapes as required. These devices can be expensive and are not typically found in small to medium-sized businesses. However, depending on the volume of data, there may be no alternative other than an autoloader or library.

Tape media is prone to failure, and tape drives require regular cleaning to maintain functionality. Tapes also have a high failure rate because they wear out through use. Tapes should only be used for a fixed amount of time before removing them from circulation. Some of the different types of tapes are:

- Digital data storage (DDS)

- Digital audio tape (DAT)

- Digital linear tape (DLT)

- Linear tape-open (LTO)

Each type has different capacities and performance characteristics.

Optical Media Discs

Optical media is a common choice for smaller amounts of data. CDs have a storage capacity of 700 MB, DVDs can support up to 8.5 GB on a single-sided dual layer disc, and HD-DVD and Blu-Ray discs can have capacities in excess of 25 GB per disc. ISPs may use optical media for transferring web content data to their customers. Customers may also use this media to transfer website content to the ISP web hosting site. Optical media can easily be accessed by any computer system with a CD or DVD drive.

Refer to **Figure** in online course

Hard Disks

Hard disk-based backup systems are becoming more and more popular because of the low cost of high-capacity drives. However, hard disks make offsite storage difficult. Large disk arrays such as direct attached storage (*DAS*), network attached storage (*NAS*), and storage area networks (*SANs*) are not transportable.

Many implementations of hard disk-based backup systems work in conjunction with tape backup systems for offsite storage. Using both hard disks and tapes in a *tiered backup* solution provides a quick restore time with the data available locally on the hard disks combined with a long-term archival solution.

Solid State Storage Devices

Solid state storage refers to all nonvolatile storage media that does not have any moving parts. Examples of solid state media range from small postage-stamp-sized drives holding 1 GB of data, to router-sized packages capable of storing 1000 GB (1TB) of data.

Solid state devices are ideal when fast storage and retrieval of data is important. Applications for solid state data storage systems include database acceleration, high-definition video access and editing, data retrieval, and SANS. High-capacity solid state storage devices can be extremely expensive, but as the technology matures, the prices will come down.

8.4.2 Methods of File Backup

Refer to **Figure** in online course

After backup media is chosen, a backup method must be selected.

Normal

A normal, or full, backup copies all selected files, in their entirety. Each file is then marked as having been backed up. With normal backups, only the most recent backup is required to restore files. This speeds up and simplifies the restore process. However, because all data is backed up, a full backup takes the most amount of time.

Differential

A *differential backup* copies only the files that have been changed since the last full backup. With differential backups, a full backup on the first day of the backup cycle is necessary. Only the files that are created or changed since the time of the last full backup are then saved. The differential backup process continues until another full backup is run. This reduces the amount of time required to perform the backup. When it is time to restore data, the last normal backup is restored and the latest differential backup restores all changed files since the last full backup.

Incremental

An *incremental backup* differs from a differential backup on one important point. Whereas a differential backup saves files that were changed since the last full backup, an incremental backup only saves files that were created or changed since the last incremental backup. This means that if an incremental backup is run every day, the backup media would only contain files created or changed on that day. Incremental backups are the quickest backup. However, they take the longest time to restore because the last normal backup and every incremental backup since the last full backup must be restored.

Refer to
Figure
in online course

Backup systems require regular maintenance to keep them running properly. There are measures that help to ensure that backups are successful:

- *Swap media -* Many backup scenarios require daily swapping of media to maintain a history of backed up data. Data loss could occur if the tape or disk is not swapped daily. Because swapping the tapes is a manual task, it is prone to failure. Users need to use a notification method, such as calendar or task scheduling.

- *Review backup logs -* Virtually all backup software produces logs. These logs report on the success of the backup or specify where it failed. Regular monitoring of backup logs allows for quick identification of any backup issues that require attention.

- *Perform trial restores -* Even if a backup logs shows that the backup was successful, there could be other problems not indicated in the log. Periodically perform a trial restore of data to verify that the backup data is usable and that the restore procedure works.

- *Perform drive maintenance -* Many backup systems require special hardware to perform backups. Tape backup systems use a tape backup drive to read and write to the tapes. Tape drives can become dirty from use and can lead to mechanical failure. Perform routine cleaning of the tape drive using designated cleaning tapes. Hard drive-based backup systems can benefit from an occasional defragmentation to improve the overall performance of the system.

Refer to
Lab Activity
for this chapter

Lab Activity

Plan a backup solution for a small business.

8.4.3 Cisco IOS Software Backup and Recovery

Refer to
Figure
in online course

In addition to backing up server files, it is also necessary for the ISP to protect configurations and the Cisco IOS software used on networking devices owned by the ISP. The Cisco networking device software and configuration files can be saved to a network server using TFTP and variations of the **copy** command. The command to save the IOS file is very similar to the command to backup and save a running configuration file.

To back up Cisco IOS software, there are three basic steps:

Step 1. Ping the TFTP server where the file should be saved. This verifies connectivity to the TFTP server. Use the **ping** command.

Step 2. On the router, verify the IOS image in flash. Use the **show flash** command to view the filename of the IOS image and file size. Confirm that the TFTP server has enough disk space to store the file.

Step 3. Copy the IOS image to the TFTP server using the command:

```
Router# copy flash tftp
```

When using the **copy** command, the router will prompt the user for the source filename, the IP address of the TFTP server, and the destination filename.

Images stored on the TFTP server can be used to restore or upgrade the Cisco IOS software on routers and switches in a network.

The steps to upgrade an IOS image file on a router are similar to the steps used to backup the file to the TFTP server. Be sure to use the **show flash** command to verify the bytes available in flash and confirm that there is enough room for the IOS file before starting the upgrade or restore.

To upgrade the Cisco IOS software, use the command:

copy tftp: flash:

When upgrading, the router will prompt the user to enter the IP address of the TFTP server followed by the filename of the image on the server that should be used. The router may prompt the user to erase the flash memory if there is not sufficient memory available for both the old and the new images. As the image is erased from flash, a series of "e"s appears to indicate the erase process. When the new image is loaded, it is verified, and the networking device is ready to be reloaded with the new Cisco IOS image.

If the IOS image is lost and must be restored, a separate process, using the ROMmon mode is required.

Refer to
Lab Activity
for this chapter

Lab Activity

Use a TFTP to backup and restore a Cisco IOS image.

Refer to
Figure
in online course

If the router is set to boot up from flash, but the Cisco IOS image in flash is erased, corrupted, or inaccessible because of lack of memory, the image may need to be restored. The quickest way to restore a Cisco IOS image to the router is by using TFTP in ROM monitor (ROMmon) mode.

The ROMmon TFTP transfer works on a specified LAN port, and defaults to the first available LAN interface. To use TFTP in ROMmon mode, the user must first set a few environmental variables, including the IP address, and then use the **tftpdnld** command to restore the image.

To set a ROMmon environment variable, type the variable name, an equal sign (=), and the value for the variable. For example, to set the IP address to 10.0.0.1, type IP_ADDRESS=10.0.0.1.

The required environment variables are:

- *IP_ADDRESS -* IP address on the LAN interface
- *IP_SUBNET_MASK -* Subnet mask for the LAN interface
- *DEFAULT_GATEWAY -* Default gateway for the LAN interface
- *TFTP_SERVER -* IP address of the TFTP server
- *TFTP_FILE -* Cisco IOS filename on the server

Use the **set** command to view and verify the ROMmon environment variables.

After the variables are set, the **tftpdnld** command is entered. As each datagram of the Cisco IOS file is received, an exclamation point (!) is displayed. As the Cisco IOS file is copied, the existing flash is erased. This includes all files that may be present in flash memory, not just the current IOS file. For this reason, it is important to back up these files to a TFTP server for safekeeping, in the event that it becomes necessary to restore the IOS image.

When the ROMmon prompt appears (rommon 1>), the router can be restarted using the **reset** command or typing **i**. The router should now boot from the new Cisco IOS image in flash.

Refer to
Lab Activity
for this chapter

Lab Activity

Use ROMmon and tftpdnld to manage an IOS image.

8.4.4 Disaster Recovery Plan

Refer to
Figure
in online course

Data backup is an important part of any disaster recovery plan. A disaster recovery plan is a comprehensive document that describes how to restore operation quickly and keep a business running during or after a disaster occurs. The objective of the disaster recovery plan is to ensure that the business can adapt to the physical and social changes that a disaster causes. A disaster can include anything from natural disasters that affect the network structure to malicious attacks on the network itself.

The disaster recovery plan can include information such as offsite locations where services can be moved, information on switching out network devices and servers, and backup connectivity options. It is important when building a disaster recovery plan to fully understand the services that are critical to maintaining operation. Services that might need to be available during a disaster include:

- Databases

- Application servers

- System management servers

- Web

- Data stores

- Directory

Refer to
Figure
in online course

When designing a disaster recovery plan, it is important to understand the needs of the organization. It is also important to gain the support necessary for a disaster recovery plan. There are several steps to accomplish designing an effective recovery plan.

- *Vulnerability assessment -* Assess how vulnerable the critical business processes and associated applications are to common disasters.

- *Risk assessment -* Analyze the risk of a disaster occurring and the associated effects and costs to the business. Part of a risk assessment is creating a list of the top-ten potential disasters and the effects, including the scenario of the business being completely destroyed.

- *Management awareness -* Use the information gathered on vulnerability and risks to get senior management approval on the disaster recovery project. Maintaining equipment and locations in the event of a possible disaster recovery could be expensive. Senior management must understand the possible effect of any disaster situation.

- *Planning group -* Establish a planning group to manage the development and implementation of the disaster recovery strategy and plan. When a disaster occurs, be it small or large scale, it is important that individuals understand their roles and responsibilities.

- *Prioritize -* Assign a priority for each disaster scenario, such as mission critical, important, or minor, for the business network, applications, and systems.

The disaster recovery planning process should first engage the top managers, and then eventually include all personnel that work with critical business processes. Everyone must be involved and support the plan for it to be successful.

Refer to
Figure
in online course

After the services and applications that are most critical to a business are identified, that information should be used to create a disaster recovery plan. There are five major phases to creating and implementing a disaster recovery plan:

Phase 1 - Network Design Recovery Strategy

Analyze the network design. Some aspects of the network design that should be included in the disaster recovery are:

- Is the network designed to survive a major disaster? Are there backup connectivity options and is there redundancy in the network design?

- Availability of offsite servers that can support applications such as email and database services.

- Availability of backup routers, switches, and other network devices should they fail.

- Location of services and resources that the network needs. Are they spread over a wide geography?

Phase 2 - Inventory and Documentation

Create an inventory of all locations, devices, vendors, used services, and contact names. Verify cost estimates that are created in the risk assessment step.

Phase 3 - Verification

Create a verification process to prove that the disaster recover strategy works. Practice disaster recovery exercises to ensure that the plan is up to date and workable.

Phase 4 - Approval and Implementation

Obtain senior management approval and develop a budget to implement the disaster recovery plan.

Phase 5 - Review

After the disaster recovery plan has been implemented for a year, review the plan.

Refer to
Interactive Graphic
in online course.

Activity

Identify the actions that are associated with each phase of creating a disaster recovery plan.

Drag each disaster recovery plan phase to the corresponding action.

Chapter Summary

Click through the buttons for summary information.

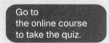

Chapter Quiz

Take the chapter quiz to check your knowledge.

Your Chapter Notes

CHAPTER 9

Troubleshooting

Introduction

Refer to
Figure
in online course

9.1 Troubleshooting Methodologies and Tools

9.1.1 The OSI Model and Troubleshooting

Refer to
Figure
in online course

One of the most important abilities for a network professional to develop is the ability to efficiently troubleshoot network problems. Good network troubleshooters are always in high demand. For this reason, Cisco certification exams measure the ability to identify and correct network problems.

When troubleshooting, many technicians use the OSI and TCP/IP networking models to help isolate the cause of a problem. Logical networking models separate network functionality into modular layers. Each layer of the OSI or TCP/IP model has specific functions and protocols. Knowledge of the features, functions, and devices of each layer, and how each layer relates to the layers around it, help a network technician to troubleshoot more efficiently.

This chapter uses the OSI and TCP/IP models to provide the structure for troubleshooting activities. Before beginning, review the material on the OSI and TCP/IP models in CCNA Discovery: Networking for Home and Small Businesses and CCNA Discovery: Working at a Small-to-Medium Business or ISP.

Refer to
Figure
in online course

OSI Reference Model as a Troubleshooting Tool

The OSI reference model provides a common language for network technicians and engineers. It is important to understand the functions that occur and the networking devices that operate at each layer of the OSI model.

The upper layers (5-7) of the OSI model deal with specific application functionality and are generally implemented only in software. Problems isolated to these layers can frequently be caused by end-system software configuration errors on clients and servers.

The lower layers (1-4) of the OSI model handle data-transport issues.

The Network Layer (Layer 3) and the Transport Layer (Layer 4) are generally implemented only in software. In addition to software errors on end systems, software configuration errors on routers and firewalls account for many problems isolated to these layers. IP addressing and routing errors occur at Layer 3.

The Physical Layer (Layer 1) and Data Link Layer (Layer 2) are implemented in both hardware and software. The Physical Layer is closest to the physical network medium, such as the network cabling, and is responsible for actually placing information on the medium. Hardware problems and incompatibilities cause most Layer 1 and Layer 2 problems.

Refer to
Interactive Graphic
in online course.

Lab Activity

Refer to
Lab Activity
for this chapter

Using the worksheet provided, organize the CCENT objectives by which layer or layers they address.

9.1.2 Troubleshooting Methodologies

Refer to **Figure** in online course

There are three main troubleshooting approaches when using network models:

- Top-down

- Bottom-up

- Divide-and-conquer

Each method assumes a layered concept of networking. Using one of these troubleshooting methods, a troubleshooter can verify all functionality at each layer until the problem is located and isolated.

Top-down - Starts with the Application Layer and works down. It looks at the problem from the point of view of the user and the application. Is it just one application that is not functioning, or do all applications fail? For example, can the user access various web pages on the Internet, but not email? Do other workstations have similar issues?

Bottom-up - Starts with the Physical Layer and works up. The Physical Layer is concerned with hardware and wire connections. Are cables securely connected? If the equipment has indicator lights, are those lights on or off?

Divide-and-Conquer - Typically troubleshooting begins at one of the middle layers and works up or down from there. For example, the troubleshooter may begin at the Network Layer by verifying IP configuration information.

The structure of these approaches makes them ideally suited for the novice troubleshooter. More experienced individuals often bypass structured approaches and rely on instinct and experience.

9.1.3 Troubleshooting Tools

Refer to **Interactive Graphic** in online course.

Refer to **Figure** in online course

It is very difficult to troubleshoot any type of network connectivity issue without a network diagram that depicts the IP addresses, IP routes, and devices, such as firewalls and switches. Logical and physical topologies are extremely useful in troubleshooting.

Physical Network Topologies

A physical network topology shows the physical layout of the devices connected to the network. Knowing how devices are physically connected is necessary for troubleshooting problems at the Physical Layer, such as cabling or hardware problems. Physical network topologies typically include:

- Device types

- Models and manufacturers of devices

- Locations

- Operating system versions

- Cable types and identifiers

- Cabling endpoints

Logical Network Topologies

A logical network topology shows how data is transferred on the network. Symbols are used to represent network elements such as routers, servers, hubs, hosts, and security devices. Logical network topologies typically include:

- Device identifiers

- IP addresses and subnet masks

- Interface identifiers

- Routing protocols

- Static and default routes

- Data-link protocols

- WAN technologies

Refer to **Figure** in online course

In addition to network diagrams, other tools may be needed to effectively troubleshoot network performance issues and failures.

Network Documentation and Baseline Tools

Network documentation and baseline tools are available for Windows, Linux, and UNIX operating systems. CiscoWorks can be used to draw network diagrams, keep network software and hardware documentation up to date, and help to cost-effectively measure baseline network bandwidth use. These software tools often provide monitoring and reporting functions for establishing the network baseline.

Network Management System Tools

Network Management System (NMS) tools monitor network performance. They graphically display a physical view of the network devices. If a failure occurs, the tool can locate the source of the failure and determine whether it was caused by malware, malicious activity, or a failed device. Examples of commonly used network management tools are CiscoView, HP Openview, Solar-Winds, and WhatsUp Gold.

Knowledge Bases

Network device vendor knowledge bases have become indispensable sources of information. When online knowledge bases are combined with Internet search engines, a network administrator has access to a vast pool of experience-based information.

Protocol Analyzers

A protocol analyzer decodes the various protocol layers in a recorded frame and presents this information in a relatively easy-to-use format. Protocol analyzers can capture network traffic for analysis. The captured output can be filtered to view specific traffic or types of traffic based on certain criteria; for example, all traffic to and from a particular device. Protocol analyzers, such as Wireshark, provide detailed troubleshooting information about the data being communicated on the network. An example of the types of information that can be viewed using a protocol analyzer is the setup and termination of a TCP session between two hosts.

Refer to **Lab Activity** for this chapter

Lab Activity

Use Wireshark to observe the TCP/IP three-way handshake.

Refer to **Figure** in online course

Sometimes failures in the lower layers of the OSI model cannot be easily identified with software tools. In these instances, it may be necessary to use hardware troubleshooting tools, such as cable testers, multimeters, and network analyzers.

Cable Testers

Cable testers are specialized, handheld devices designed for testing the various types of data communication cabling. Cable testers can be used to detect broken wires, crossed-over wiring, shorted connections, and improperly paired connections. More sophisticated testers, such as a time-domain reflectometer (TDR), can pinpoint the distance to a break in a cable. Cable testers can also determine the length of a cable.

Digital Multimeters

Digital multimeters (DMMs) are test instruments that directly measure electrical values of voltage, current, and resistance. In network troubleshooting, most of the multimeter tests involve checking power-supply voltage levels and verifying that network devices are receiving power.

Portable Network Analyzers

By plugging a network analyzer into a switch anywhere on the network, a network engineer can see the average and peak utilization of the segment. The analyzer can also be used to identify the devices producing the most network traffic, analyze network traffic by protocol, and view interface details. Network analyzers are useful when troubleshooting problems caused by malware or denial-of-service attacks.

9.1.4 Certification Study Guide

Refer to
Lab Activity
for this chapter

CCENT Study Guide

Click the lab icon to download a CCENT Preparation Guide for section 9.1.

Click the lab icon to download a CCENT Preparation Guide.

9.2 Troubleshooting Layer 1 and Layer 2 Issues

9.2.1 Layer 1 and 2 Problems

Refer to
Figure
in online course

The Physical and the Data Link Layers encompass both hardware and software functions. All network communications rely on the technologies at these layers to function. A network technician must be able to quickly isolate and correct problems occurring at these layers.

The Physical Layer, or Layer 1, is responsible for the physical and electrical specifications for the transmission of bits from one host to another over the physical medium, either wired or wireless. Network problems occurring at Layer 1 can cause the loss of network connectivity, or simply cause network performance to degrade.

The types of problems that occur at Layer 1 are directly related to the type of technology used. For example, Ethernet is a multi-access technology. Ethernet protocols use an algorithm to sense when there are no other signals on the wire to begin a transmission. However, it is possible for two devices to begin sending at the exact same time, causing a collision. When a collision occurs, all devices stop transmitting and wait a random amount of time before transmitting again. Because Ethernet can detect collisions and respond to them, Ethernet is often referred to as Carrier Sense Multiple Access with Collision Detection (CSMA/CD).

However, excessive collisions can cause network performance to degrade. Collisions can be a significant problem on shared media, such as a hub network, more so than on switched ports.

Refer to
Figure
in online course

The Data Link Layer, or Layer 2, specifies how the data is formatted for transmission over the network media. It also regulates how access to the network is granted. Layer 2 provides the link between the Network Layer software functions and the Layer 1 hardware for both LAN and WAN applications. To effectively troubleshoot Layer 1 and Layer 2 problems, technicians must be familiar with cabling standards, and encapsulation and framing.

After a technician verifies that Layer 1 is functioning, it must be determined if the problem resides in Layer 2 or one of the higher layers. For example, if a host can ping the local loopback address, 127.0.0.1, but cannot access any services over the network, the problem may be isolated to Layer 2 framing issues or a misconfigured interface card. Network analyzers and other online tools can locate the source of a Layer 2 issue. In some instances, a device recognizes that a Layer 2 problem occurred and sends alert messages to the console.

Activity

Match the Layer 1 or Layer 2 cause with the possible symptom.

Drag the cause to the appropriate symptom box.

Refer to
Interactive Graphic
in online course.

9.2.2 Troubleshooting Device Hardware and Boot Errors

Refer to
Figure
in online course

Network problems often occur after a device is restarted. Restarts can happen intentionally after an upgrade, or unexpectedly after a power failure. To troubleshoot device hardware failures and boot errors, it is first necessary to review the process that Cisco IOS devices use during startup. The bootup process has three stages:

1. Performing the POST and loading the bootstrap program.

2. Locating and loading the Cisco IOS software.

3. Locating and loading the startup configuration file or entering setup mode.

When booting any Cisco networking device, it is helpful to observe the console messages that appear during the boot sequence. After the Cisco IOS software is loaded, the technician can use commands to verify that the hardware and software are fully operational.

The `show version` command displays the version of the operating system and whether all interface hardware is recognized.

The `show flash` command displays the contents of the Flash memory, including the Cisco IOS image file. It also displays the amount of Flash memory currently being used and the amount of memory available.

The `show ip interfaces brief` command shows the operational status of the device interfaces and IP addresses assigned.

The `show running-configuration` and `show startup-configuration` commands verify whether all the configuration commands were recognized during the reload.

When a device fails to boot correctly and creates a network outage, replace the device with a known good device to restore services to end users. After service is restored, then take the time to troubleshoot and repair the failed device.

Refer to
Figure
in online course

After a router boots successfully, the green LED indicators will display. When errors occur during the bootup process, Cisco devices execute default actions to recover from the errors, such as loading into ROMmon mode. There are five common bootup errors (discussed on this page and the next), that have associated troubleshooting strategies.

Device Fails POST

When a device fails POST, no output appears on the console screen. In addition, system LEDs may change color or blink, depending on the device type. For a description of LED operation, check the documentation provided with the device. If the POST fails, turn off the power, unplug the device, and remove all interface modules. Then reboot the device. If the POST still fails, the device requires service. If it completes the POST successfully without the interface modules installed, an interface module may have failed. Disconnect the power and reinstall each module individually, rebooting each time, to determine which module has failed. When the failed module is identified, replace it with a known good module and restart the device.

Cisco IOS Image in Flash is Corrupt

If the image file in flash is corrupt or missing, the bootloader cannot find a valid Cisco IOS file to load. Some Cisco IOS devices have an image with limited functionality that is loaded and run if no image exists in flash or another specified location. This image is called a boothelper. Boothelper images may not have enough functionality to successfully execute the necessary configuration commands to bring the device back into operation. If there is no boothelper, the device enters ROMmon mode. Use ROMmon commands to reload the correct Cisco IOS image from a TFTP server.

Refer to
Figure
in online course

Memory is not Recognized or Fails

If there is not enough memory to decompress the image, the device scrolls error messages rapidly or constantly reboots. The device may be able to boot into ROMmon mode by issuing a `Ctrl-Break` command during startup. In ROMmon mode, commands can be issued to determine the status of the memory. The memory may have to be replaced or increased for the device to function normally.

Interface Modules are not Recognized

Faulty or improperly seated interface modules may not be recognized during the POST and Cisco IOS load. When this occurs, the list of available interfaces displayed by the show version command does not match the physically installed modules. If an interface module is new, check that the module is supported by the Cisco IOS version that is installed and that enough memory exists to support the module. Always power down the device, disconnect the power, and reseat the module into the device to determine if there is a hardware problem. After reseating, if the module is not recognized during reboot, replace it with a known good module.

Configuration File is Corrupt or Missing

If a valid startup configuration file cannot be found, some Cisco devices execute an autoinstall utility. This utility broadcasts a TFTP request for a configuration file. Other devices immediately enter an initial configuration dialog, known as the setup utility or setup mode. Devices that have the autoinstall utility also enter setup mode if no TFTP server responds after five inquiries. Use either TFTP or manual configuration to reload or recreate the configuration. Devices do not forward traffic until a valid configuration is loaded.

9.2.3 Troubleshooting Cable and Device Port Errors

Refer to
Figure
in online course

Router interface errors are often the first symptom of Layer 1 and Layer 2 cabling or connectivity errors. To troubleshoot, begin by examining the statistics recorded on the problematic interface using the `show interfaces` command and the status of interfaces using the `show ip interface brief` command.

The output for the `show ip interface brief` command includes a summary of the device interfaces, including the IP address and interface status.

- *Up/up status* - indicates normal operation and that both the media and the Layer 2 protocol are functional.

- *Down/down status* - indicates that a connectivity or media problem exists.

- *Up/down status -* indicates that the media is connected properly, but that the Layer 2 protocol is not functioning or is misconfigured.

Common cable or media issues that can cause a down/down output include:

- Loose cable or too much tension on the cable - If all the pins cannot make a good connection, the circuit is down.

- Incorrect termination - Ensure that the correct standard is followed and that all pins are correctly terminated in the connector.

- Damaged serial interface connector - Pins on the interface connection are bent or missing.

- Break or short in the cable - If there are problems along the circuit, the interface cannot sense the correct signals.

Common Layer 2 issues that can cause an up/down output include:

- Encapsulation is improperly configured.

- No keepalives are received on the interface.

Occasionally, media errors are not severe enough to cause the circuit to fail, but do cause network performance issues. The `show interfaces` command provides additional troubleshooting information to help identify these media errors.

Output for the `show interfaces` command includes:

- *Excessive Noise -* On Ethernet and serial interfaces, the presence of many CRC errors but not many collisions is an indication of excessive noise. CRC errors usually indicate a media or cable error. Common causes include electrical interference, loose or damaged connections, or using the incorrect cabling type.

- *Excessive collisions -* Collisions usually occur only on half-duplex or shared-media Ethernet connections. Damaged cables can cause excessive collisions.

- *Excessive runt frames -* Malfunctioning NICs are the usual cause of runt frames, but they can be caused by the same issues as excessive collisions.

- *Late collisions -* A properly designed and configured network should never have late collisions. Excessive cable lengths are the most common cause. Duplex mismatches can also be responsible.

Lab Activity

Use the `show ip interface brief` and `show interfaces` commands to identify possible cable or media errors.

9.2.4 Troubleshooting LAN Connectivity Issues

LAN troubleshooting usually centers on switches, because the majority of LAN users connect to the network via switch ports. Many of the same Cisco IOS `show` commands can be used on switches to gather troubleshooting information. In addition, each port on a switch has an LED indicator that provides valuable troubleshooting information.

The first step in troubleshooting LAN connectivity issues is to verify that the switch port connected to the user is active and that the appropriate LED indicators are lit. If there is physical access to the switch, it can save time to look at the port LEDs, which give the link status or indicate an error condition (if red or orange). Check to see that both sides of the connection have a link.

If no link light is present, ensure that the cable is connected at both ends and that it is connected to the correct port. Make sure that both devices are powered up, and that there are no bootup errors on either device. Swap out any patch cables with known good cables and verify that the cable terminations are correct for the type of connectivity desired. If there is still no link light, verify that the port is not administratively shut down. Use the **show running-config interface** command to show the parameters configured on a switch port:

Refer to
Figure
in online course

```
Switch#sh run interface fastEthernet 4/2
 !
 interface FastEthernet4/2
  shutdown
  duplex full
  speed 100
end
```

Even if a link light is present, it does not guarantee that the cable is fully functional. The cable can be damaged, causing intermittent performance problems. Normally, this situation is identified by using Cisco IOS **show** commands to determine if the port has many packet errors, or if the port constantly flaps (loses and regains a link).

The **show version** and **show interfaces** commands executed on a switch provide similar information to the same commands executed on a router. To get a quick view of switch port error statistics, use the **show interfaceportcounters errors** command.

Duplex mismatches are more common on switches than on routers. Many devices are set to autonegotiate speed and duplex settings. If one device on a link is configured to autonegotiate and the other side is manually configured with speed and duplex settings, mismatches may occur, leading to collisions and dropped packets.

To view the speed and duplex settings on a port and whether manual or autonegotiation features were used, use the **show interfaceportstatus** command.

If the mismatch occurs between two Cisco devices with the Cisco Discovery Protocol (CDP) enabled, there are CDP error messages on the console or in the logging buffer of both devices. CDP is useful to detect errors and port and system statistics on nearby Cisco devices.

To correct duplex mismatch errors, set both devices to autonegotiate speed and duplex. If the negotiation does not produce the desired results, manually configure matching speed and duplex settings on each device.

Refer to **Packet
Tracer Activity**
for this chapter

Packet Tracer Activity

Configure a switched network and troubleshoot duplex mismatches.

Refer to
Lab Activity
for this chapter

Lab Activity

Troubleshoot LAN connectivity using LEDs and show commands.

9.2.5 Troubleshooting WAN Connectivity Issues

Refer to
Figure
in online course

Troubleshooting a serial WAN connection is different from troubleshooting Ethernet LAN connections. Typically, WAN connectivity relies on equipment and media that is owned and managed by a telecommunications service provider (TSP). Because of this, it is important for technicians to know how to troubleshoot the customer premises equipment and to communicate the results to the TSP.

Most serial interface and line problems can be identified and corrected using information gathered from the **show interfaces serial** command. Serial connections may experience problems caused by packet errors, configuration errors, or mismatches in encapsulation and timing. Because serial WAN connections usually rely on a CSU/DSU or modem for timing, these devices must be considered when troubleshooting serial lines. In prototype networks, a router can be configured to provide DCE clocking functions, eliminating the CSU or modem.

To successfully troubleshoot serial WAN connectivity problems, it is important to know the type of modem or CSU/DSU that is installed and how to place the device in a loopback state for testing.

Refer to
Figure
in online course

The interface status line of the **show interfaces serial** command can display six possible problem states:

- **Serial _x_ is down, line protocol is down (DTE mode)** - When the router serial interface cannot detect any signal on the line, it reports both the line and the Layer 2 protocol down.

- **Serial _x_ is up, line protocol is down (DTE mode)** - If the serial interface does not receive keepalives or if there is an encapsulation error, the Layer 2 protocol is reported down.

- **Serial _x_ is up, line protocol is down (DCE mode)** - In cases where the router is providing the clock signal and a DCE cable is attached, but no clock rate is configured, the Layer 2 protocol is reported down.

- **Serial _x_ is up, line protocol is up (looped)** - It is common practice to place a circuit in a loopback condition to test connectivity. If the serial interface receives its own signals back on the circuit, it reports the line as looped.

- **Serial _x_ is up, line protocol is down (disabled)** - High error rates cause the router to place the line in a protocol disabled mode. This type of problem is usually hardware related.

- **Serial _x_ is administratively down, line protocol is down** - An administratively down interface is one that is configured with the **shutdown** command. Usually all that is needed to fix this condition is to enter the **no shutdown** command on the interface. If the interface does not come up using the **no shutdown** command, check the console messages for a duplicate IP address message. If a duplicate IP address exists, correct the problem and issue the **no shutdown** command again.

- **Serial _x_ is up, line protocol is up** - The interface is operating as expected.

Refer to **Packet Tracer Activity** for this chapter

Packet Tracer Activity

Troubleshoot WAN encapsulation mismatches.

Refer to **Lab Activity** for this chapter

Lab Activity

Troubleshoot WAN connectivity using LEDs and show commands.

9.2.6 Certification Study Guide

Refer to **Lab Activity** for this chapter

CCENT Study Guide

Click the lab icon to download a CCENT Preparation Guide for section 9.2.

Click the lab icon to download a CCENT Preparation Guide.

9.3 Troubleshooting Layer 3 IP Addressing Issues
9.3.1 Review of Layer 3 Functionality and IP Addressing

Refer to
Figure
in online course

Layer 1 networks are created by interconnecting devices using physical media. Layer 2 network protocols are hardware dependent. Ethernet cannot operate over a serial link, nor can serial communications occur using an Ethernet NIC.

Layer 3 (the Network Layer) protocols are not bound to a specific type of media or Layer 2 framing protocol. The same Layer 3 protocols can operate on Ethernet, wireless, serial, or other Layer 2 networks. Layer 3 networks can contain hosts that are connected using different Layer 1 and 2 technologies. The primary functions implemented at Layer 3 of the OSI model are network addressing and routing. Layer 3 networks are referred to as logical networks because they are created only in software.

Today most networks implement the TCP/IP protocols to exchange information between hosts. As a result, much of the focus of troubleshooting Layer 3 problems is concentrated on IP addressing errors and on routing protocol operation.

Troubleshooting Layer 3 problems requires a thorough understanding of network boundaries and IP addressing. Poorly designed and configured IP addressing schemes account for a large number of network performance problems.

Refer to
Figure
in online course

At Layer 3, each packet must be identified with the source and destination addresses of the two end systems. With IPv4, each packet has a 32-bit source address and a 32-bit destination address in the Layer 3 header.

The IP address identifies not only the individual host, but also the Layer 3 local network on which the host can communicate. A simple IP network can be created by configuring two interconnected hosts with unique addresses that share the same network prefix and subnet mask.

A device must be configured with an IP address to exchange messages using TCP/IP. Individual Layer 3 IP networks encompass a range of IP addresses. These boundaries are determined by the number of bits contained in the network prefix portion of the address. A simple rule is the longer the network prefix, the smaller the range of IP addresses that can be configured on hosts in that IP network.

To troubleshoot Layer 3 problems, an administrator must be able to determine the range of host addresses that belong to each individual IP network. The range of addresses is determined by the number and position of host bits. For example, in a 192.168.1.0/24 network, borrow three bits for subnetting. This leaves 5 bits for host addresses. This creates 8 subnets ($2^3=8$) and 30 hosts per subnet ($2^5 - 2 = 30$).

Given the 192.168.1.96/27 subnet, the first host on the subnet will be 192.168.1.97, and the last host will be 192.168.1.126. The broadcast address for this subnet will be 192.168.1.127. This can be seen by looking at the binary of the last octet:

(011 subnet) 96 + (00001 first host) 1 = (01100001) 97 in decimal

(011 subnet) 96 + (11110 last host) 30 = (01111110) 126

(011 subnet) 96 + (11111 broadcast) 31 = (01111111) 127

This example is using a class C address. This same technique can be applied to Class A and Class B addresses. Remember that the location of host bits can extend into more than one octet.

Refer to
Interactive Graphic
in online course.

Packet Tracer Activity

Troubleshoot a small network.

Refer to **Packet
Tracer Activity**
for this chapter

9.3.2 IP Design and Configuration Issues

Refer to
Figure
in online course

If IP addressing is assigned in a random manner, it is difficult to determine where a source or destination address is located. Today, most networks employ a hierarchical IP addressing scheme. Hierarchical IP addressing schemes offer many advantages, including smaller routing tables that require less processing power. Hierarchical IP addressing also creates a more structured environment that is easier to document, troubleshoot, and expand.

However, a poorly planned hierarchical network, or a badly documented plan, can create problems, such as overlapping subnets or incorrectly configured subnet masks on devices. These two conditions account for many IP addressing and routing issues within networks.

An overlapping subnet occurs when the address range of two separate subnets include some of the same host or broadcast addresses. Overlapping is usually a result of poor network documentation or by accidentally entering the incorrect subnet mask or network prefix. Overlapping subnets do not always cause a complete network outage. They may only affect a few hosts, depending on where the misconfigured subnet mask is placed.

Refer to
Figure
in online course

Cisco IOS software does permit you to configure an IP address from overlapping subnets on two different interfaces. However, the router does not activate the second interface.

For example, the router R1 interface Fast Ethernet 0/0 is configured with an IP address and subnet mask on the 192.168.1.0/24 network. If Fast Ethernet 0/1 is configured with an IP address on the 192.168.1.0/30 network, an overlapping error message appears. If there is an attempt to enable the interface with the `no shutdown` command, a second error message appears. No traffic is forwarded through the interface. The output from the `show ip interface brief` command shows that the second interface configured for the 192.168.1.0/24 network, FastEthernet 0/1, is down.

It is important to verify the status of the interfaces after making configuration changes. An interface that remains administratively down after the `no shutdown` command is issued can indicate an IP addressing problem.

Refer to
Figure
in online course

Although Cisco IOS software has safeguards to ensure that overlapping subnets are not configured on multiple interfaces of the same device, it does not prevent overlapping subnets from being configured on different devices or on hosts within the network.

A poorly configured subnet mask can cause some hosts on a network to not have access to network services. Subnet mask configuration errors can also present a variety of symptoms that may not be easily identified.

Refer to
Interactive Graphic
in online course.

Refer to
Figure
in online course

9.3.3 IP Address Planning and Allocation Issues

Poor address allocation planning can cause other problems. Often, an administrator underestimates the potential for growth when designing subnets. As a result, the IP subnetting scheme does not allow for enough host addresses in each subnet. One indication of a subnet having too many hosts is when some hosts are unable to receive an IP address from the DHCP server.

When a host running Microsoft Windows does not receive an address from a DHCP server, it automatically assigns itself an address on the 169.254.0.0 network. If this occurs, use the `show ip dhcp binding` command to check whether the DHCP server has available addresses .

Another indication of not enough IP addresses is an error message on a host stating that duplicate IP addresses exist. If a host device is turned off when the DHCP lease expires, the address is returned to the DHCP pool and can be issued to another host. When the original lease holder is turned back on, it requests a renewal of its previous IP address. In a Microsoft Windows network, both hosts report a duplicate IP address error.

Refer to **Interactive Graphic** in online course.

Refer to **Lab Activity** for this chapter

Refer to **Figure** in online course

Lab Activity

Create an IP addressing scheme that allows for 20% growth in the number of attached hosts.

9.3.4 DHCP and NAT Issues

DHCP can create another level of complication when troubleshooting network issues. If hosts are configured to use DHCP and are not able to connect to the network, verify that IP addressing is assigned using the Windows command, **ipconfig /all**. If hosts are not receiving IP addressing assignments, it is necessary to troubleshoot the DHCP configuration.

Regardless of whether the DHCP service is configured on a dedicated server or on the router, the first step in troubleshooting is to check the physical connectivity. If a separate server is used, check that the server is receiving network traffic. If the DHCP service is configured on a router, use the **show interfaces** command on the router to confirm that the interface is operational. If the interface connected to the host network is down, the port does not pass traffic, including DHCP requests.

Next, verify that the DHCP server is correctly configured and has available IP addresses to lease. After this is confirmed, check for any address conflicts. Address conflicts can occur even if there are available addresses within the DHCP pool. This can happen if a host is statically configured with an address that is also contained in the range of the DHCP pool.

Use the **show ip dhcp conflict** command to display all address conflicts recorded by the DHCP server. If an address conflict is detected, the address is removed from the pool and not assigned until an administrator resolves the conflict.

If none of these steps diagnoses the problem, test to ensure that the issue is actually with DHCP. Configure a host with a static IP address, subnet mask, and default gateway. If the workstation is unable to reach network resources with a statically configured IP address, the root cause of the problem is not DHCP. At this point, network connectivity troubleshooting is required.

Refer to **Figure** in online course

DHCP is a broadcast protocol, which means that the DHCP server must be reachable through a broadcast message. Because routers normally do not forward broadcasts, either the DHCP server must be on the same local network as the hosts or the router must be configured to relay the broadcast messages.

A router can be configured to forward all broadcast packets, including DHCP requests, to a specific server using the **ip helper-address** command. This command allows a router to change the destination broadcast addresses within a packet to a specified *unicast* address:

```
Router(config-if)# ip helper-address x.x.x.x
```

Once this command is configured, all broadcast packets will be forwarded to the server IP address specified in the command, including DHCP requests.

When a router forwards address requests, it is acting as a DHCP relay agent. If DHCP relay is not operational, no hosts can obtain an IP address. When no hosts can obtain an IP address from a DHCP server that is located on another network, verify that the helper address is configured correctly on the router.

Refer to **Figure** in online course

If the hosts on the internal network are assigned private addresses, NAT is required to communicate with the public network. Usually the first indication that there is a NAT problem is that users cannot reach sites located on the Internet. There are three types of address translation: static, dynamic, and PAT. Two common types of configuration errors affect all three translation methods.

Incorrect Designation of Inside and Outside Interfaces

It is critical that the correct interfaces are designated as the inside or outside interface for NAT. In most NAT implementations, the inside interface connects to the local network, which uses private IP address space. The outside interface connects to the public network, usually the ISP. Verify this configuration using the `show running-config interface` command.

Incorrect Assignment of Interface IP Address or Pool Addresses

In most NAT implementations, the IP address pool and static NAT translation entries must use IP addresses that are on the same local IP network as the outside interface. If not, addresses are translated, but no route to the translated addresses are found. Check the configuration to verify that all the translated addresses are reachable. When the address translation is configured to use the outside interface address in PAT, make sure that the interface address is on the correct network and is configured with the proper subnet mask.

Another common issue is that when dynamic NAT or PAT is enabled, external users are no longer able to connect to internal devices. If external users must be able to reach specific servers on the internal network, be sure that static translations are configured.

Refer to
Figure
in online course

If you are certain that NAT is configured correctly, it is important to verify that NAT is operational.

One of the most useful commands when verifying NAT operation is the `show ip nat translations` command. After viewing the existing translations, clear them using the `clear ip nat translation *` command. Be aware that clearing all IP translations on a router may disrupt user services. Then use the `show ip nat translations` command again. If new translations appear, there may be another problem causing the loss of Internet connectivity.

Verify that there is a route to the Internet for the translated addresses. Use `traceroute` to determine the path the translated packets are taking and verify that the route is correct. Also, if possible, trace the route to a translated address from a remote device on the outside network. This can help isolate the next troubleshooting target. There may be a routing problem on the router where the trace output stops.

Refer to **Packet Tracer Activity** for this chapter

Packet Tracer Activity

Use `show` commands to troubleshoot DHCP and NAT.

9.3.5 Certification Study Guide

Refer to **Lab Activity** for this chapter

CCENT Study Guide

Click the lab icon to download a CCENT Preparation Guide for section 9.3.

Click the lab icon to download a CCENT Preparation Guide.

9.4 Troubleshooting Layer 3 Routing Issues

9.4.1 Layer 3 Routing Issues

Refer to
Figure
in online course

Layer 3 encompasses the addressing of networks and hosts, and the protocols that route packets between networks.

Most networks have a number of different types of routes, including a combination of static, dynamic, and default routes. Problems with routing can cause network failures or adversely affect network performance. These problems can be the result of manual route entry errors, routing protocol configuration and operation errors, or failures at lower layers of the OSI model.

To troubleshoot Layer 3 problems, it is important to understand how routing works, including how each type of route functions and is configured.

You may want to review the materials and activities in CCNA Discovery: Networking for Home and Small Businesses and CCNA Discovery: Working at a Small-to-Medium Business or ISP on routing and routing protocols before continuing with this chapter.

Refer to
Figure
in online course

The status of a network can change frequently for a variety of reasons, including:

- An interface fails.

- A service provider drops a connection.

- The available bandwidth is overloaded.

- An administrator enters an incorrect configuration.

When there is a change in the network status, routes can be lost, or an incorrect route can be installed into the routing table.

The primary tool to use when troubleshooting Layer 3 routing problems is the `show ip route` command. This command displays all the routes the router uses to forward traffic. The routing table consists of route entries from the following sources:

- Directly connected networks

- Static routes

- Dynamic routing protocols

Routing protocols choose which routes are preferred based on route metrics. Directly connected networks have a metric of 0, static routes also have a default metric of 0, and dynamic routes have various routing metrics, depending on the routing protocol used.

If there is more than one route to a specific destination network, the route with the lowest administrative distance (AD) is installed into the routing table.

Any time a routing problem is suspected, use the `show ip route` command to ensure that all the expected routes are installed in the routing table.

Refer to
Figure
in online course

Connected Route Problems

Directly connected routes are automatically installed in the routing table when an IP address is configured on an interface, and the interface is enabled using the `no shutdown` command. If a directly connected route does not appear in the table, use the `show interfaces` or `show ip interface brief` command to verify that an address is assigned and that the interface is in an up/up state.

Static and Default Route Problems

When a static or default route does not appear in the routing table, the problem is most likely a configuration error. Static and default routes must use either an exit interface or the IP address of a next hop router. Static routing errors sometimes occur because the next hop address is not in the correct IP address range of any directly connected network. Verify that the configuration statements are correct and that the exit interfaces used by the routes are in an up/up state.

Dynamic Route Problems

There are many different types of problems that can cause dynamic routes to not appear in the routing table. Because dynamic routing protocols exchange route tables with all other routers in the network, a missing route could be caused by a misconfiguration on one or more of the routers on the path to the destination.

Refer to **Packet Tracer Activity** for this chapter

Packet Tracer Activity

Use routing table principles to solve a routing problem.

9.4.2 Dynamic Routing Errors

Refer to **Figure** in online course

Routing table updates usually occur when a new network is configured or an already configured network becomes unreachable.

If directly connected routes appear in the router table, the routing table is accessed and changed only if the directly connected interface changes states. If static or default routes are configured, the routing table changes only if new routes are specified or if the exit interface specified in the static or default route changes states.

Dynamic routing protocols automatically send updates to other routers in the network. If dynamic routing is enabled, a router accesses and changes its own routing table any time a change is reported in an update from a neighboring router.

RIP is a dynamic routing protocol used in small- to medium-sized LANs. When troubleshooting issues specific to RIP, check the versioning and configuration statements.

It is always best to use the same version of the routing protocol on all routers. Although RIPv1 and RIPv2 are compatible, RIPv1 does not support classless routing or variable length subnet masks (VLSM). This can create issues if both RIPv1 and RIPv2 are configured to run on the same network. Additionally, while RIPv2 automatically listens for both RIPv1 and RIPv2 updates from neighbors, RIPv1 does not listen for RIPv2 updates.

Routing problems also occur if there are incorrect or missing network statements. The network statement does two things:

■ It enables the routing protocol to send and receive updates on any local interfaces that belong to that network.

■ It includes that network in its routing updates to its neighboring routers.

A missing or incorrect network statement results in inaccurate routing updates and can prevent an interface from sending or receiving routing updates.

Refer to **Figure** in online course

Many tools exist for troubleshooting dynamic routing issues.

TCP/IP utilities, such as ping and traceroute, are used to verify connectivity. Telnet can be used to verify connectivity and make configuration changes. Cisco IOS show commands display a snapshot of a configuration or the status of a particular component. The Cisco IOS command set also includes various debug commands.

Debug commands are dynamic and provide real-time information on traffic movement and the interaction of protocols. For example, the `debug ip rip` command displays the exchange of RIP routing updates and packets as they occur.

Debug functions use a significant portion of CPU resources and can slow or stop normal router operations. For this reason, use debug commands to isolate problems, not to monitor normal network operation.

Refer to **Packet Tracer Activity** for this chapter

Packet Tracer Activity

Subnet an address space, configure devices, and use combination of RIPv2 and static routing to provide connectivity between remote hosts.

Refer to **Lab Activity** for this chapter

Lab Activity

Troubleshoot a RIP router network configured with errors.

9.4.3 Certification Study Guide

Refer to
Lab Activity
for this chapter

CCENT Study Guide

Click the lab icon to download a CCENT Preparation Guide for section 9.4.

Click the lab icon to download a CCENT Preparation Guide.

9.5 Troubleshooting Layer 4 and Upper Layer Issues

9.5.1 Layer 4 Traffic Filtering Errors

Refer to
Figure
in online course

Layer 4, the Transport Layer, is considered a transition between the upper and lower layers of the OSI model. Layer 4 is responsible for transporting data packets and specifies the port number used to reach specific applications. Layer 4 network problems can arise at the edge of the network where security technologies are examining and modifying the traffic. Many problems are caused by firewalls that are configured to deny traffic based on port numbers, even though this traffic should be forwarded.

Layer 4 supports both UDP and TCP traffic. Some applications use TCP, some use UDP, and some use both. When denying traffic based on the port number, it is necessary to specify the transport protocol used. Some engineers are unsure of which transport protocol is used by specific applications and therefore deny the port number for both TCP and UDP traffic. This practice may unexpectedly deny traffic that should be allowed.

Firewalls are also often configured to deny everything except the applications specified in the permit statements. If traffic that should be permitted is not included in the firewall statements, or if a new application is added to the network without a corresponding permission being added to the firewall, filtering problems occur.

A common indication of Layer 4 problems is users reporting that some web services, especially video or audio, are not reachable.

Verify that the ports being permitted and denied by the firewall are the correct ones for the applications. For a better understanding of which ports correspond to specific applications, review the information on TCP, UDP, and ports in CCNA Discovery: Networking for Home and Small Businesses and CCNA Discovery: Working at a Small-to-Medium Business or ISP.

Refer to
Interactive Graphic
in online course.

9.5.2 Troubleshooting Upper Layer Problems

Refer to
Figure
in online course

Most of the upper layer protocols provide user services that are typically used for network management, file transfer, distributed file services, terminal emulation, and email. Protocols at these layers are often referred to as TCP/IP Application Layer protocols, because the TCP/IP model Application Layer encompasses the upper three layers of the OSI model.

The most widely known and implemented TCP/IP Application Layer protocols include:

- Telnet - Enables users to establish terminal session connections with remote hosts.

- HTTP - Supports the exchange of text, graphic images, sound, video, and other multimedia files on the web.

- FTP - Performs interactive file transfers between hosts, using TCP.

- TFTP - Performs basic interactive file transfers typically between hosts and networking devices, using UDP .

- SMTP - Supports basic email message delivery services.

- POP3 - Connects to mail servers and downloads email to a client application.

- IMAP4 - Enables email clients to retrieve messages and store email on servers.

- SNMP - Collects information from managed devices.

- NTP - Provides updated time to hosts and network devices.

- DNS - Maps IP addresses to the names assigned to hosts.

- SSL - Provides encryption and security for HTTP transactions.

- SSH - Provides secure remote terminal access to servers and networking devices.

> Refer to
> **Figure**
> in online course

It can be difficult to isolate problems to the upper layers, especially if the client configuration does not reveal any obvious problems. To determine that a network problem is with an upper layer function, start by eliminating basic connectivity as the source of the problem.

Using the "divide and conquer" method of troubleshooting, begin with verifying Layer 3 connectivity.

Step 1. Ping the host default gateway.

Step 2. Verify end-to-end connectivity.

Step 3. Verify the routing configuration.

Step 4. Ensure that NAT is working correctly.

Step 5. Check for firewall filter rules.

If the problem exists on a remote network, end-to-end connectivity cannot be verified because there is no control over all the connections. For this reason, it is possible that even though the configurations on the local devices are correct, there is still a problem with the remote network. Be sure to check with the ISP to ensure that their network connection is up and operational.

If all these steps are completed successfully, and it is verified that the end-to-end connectivity is not the issue, but the end device is still not operating as expected, the problem has been isolated to the upper layers.

> Refer to
> **Figure**
> in online course

Upper layer problems prevent services from being provided to application programs. A problem at the upper layers can result in unreachable or unusable resources, even when the lower layers are functional. It is possible to have full network connectivity, but the application cannot provide data.

Problems with upper layer functions usually affect just a few applications, perhaps even only one. It is not unusual for a help desk technician to get a call from a user who cannot receive email, although all other applications are functioning correctly.

Misconfigured client applications account for the majority of upper layer network problems. When an incorrect email or FTP server is specified, the client cannot find and retrieve information. When more than one application is affected, the upper layer problem may be attributed to a DNS server issue.

To verify that DNS is functioning correctly and can resolve server addresses, use the Windows command **nslookup**. If DNS is not working as expected, ensure that the correct DNS server address is configured on the host. When hosts receive DNS server information from a DHCP server, verify that the DHCP server has the correct IP address for the DNS server.

If the DNS server is operational and reachable, check for DNS zone configuration errors. Look for a typographical error in an address or name within the files.

Refer to
Figure
in online course

The upper layers are responsible for encryption and compression. A mismatch between the way a client encrypts or compresses the data and the way the server interprets it can cause applications to not function or to function poorly.

When a problem occurs on a single host or workstation, it may be a problem with the way the information is being interpreted in the host software. Browser plug-in programs, such as Adobe Reader, often perform upper layer functions. These programs must be kept updated for web pages to display correctly.

Using an incorrect protocol to request data can cause a web page to be unreachable. For example, it may be necessary to specify **https://** on the browser address line, rather than **http://** to retrieve an SSL-protected web page.

9.5.3 Using Telnet to Check Upper Layer Connectivity

Refer to
Figure
in online course

Telnet is an excellent tool to use when troubleshooting problems with upper layer functions. Using Telnet to access the networking devices enables the technician to enter commands on each device as if they were locally attached. In addition, the ability to reach devices using Telnet indicates that the lower layer connectivity exists between the devices.

However, Telnet is an insecure protocol, which means that all data communicated can be captured and read. If there is a possibility that communications can be intercepted by unauthorized users, Secure Shell (SSH) protocol should be used instead. SSH is a more secure method for remote device access.

Most newer versions of the Cisco IOS software contain an SSH server. In some devices, this service is enabled by default. Other devices require the SSH server to be manually enabled.

Cisco IOS devices also include an SSH client that can be used to establish SSH sessions with other devices. Similarly, a remote computer with an SSH client can be used to start a secure CLI session. SSH client software is not provided by default on all computer operating systems. The technician may need to acquire, install, and configure SSH client software on the computer.

Review the material in CCNA Discovery: Working at a Small-to-Medium Business or ISP on configuring and using SSH.

Refer to
Lab Activity
for this chapter

Lab Activity

Access networking devices using Telnet and SSH.

9.5.4 Certification Study Guide

Refer to
Lab Activity
for this chapter

CCENT Study Guide

Click the lab icon to download a CCENT Preparation Guide for section 9.5.

Click the lab icon to download a CCENT Preparation Guide.

9.6 Preparing for Cisco Certification

9.6.1 Knowledge, Skills and Abilities

Refer to
Figure
in online course

The Cisco Certified Entry Networking Technician (CCENT) certification validates the skills required for entry-level network support positions, the starting point for many successful careers in networking. CCENT certification is the first step toward achieving CCNA certification (Cisco Certified Network Associate), which covers medium-size enterprise branch networks that have more complex connections. To obtain CCENT certification, a candidate must pass the ICND1 examination at a Cisco Certified Testing Center.

The ICND1 exam (640-822) tests the ability to install, operate, and troubleshoot a small branch office network. The exam includes topics on networking fundamentals:

- Connecting to a WAN

- Basic security and wireless concepts

- Routing and switching

- TCP/IP and OSI models

- IP addressing

- WAN technologies

- Operating and configuring Cisco IOS devices

- Configuring RIPv2, static and default routing

- Implementing NAT and DHCP

- Configuring simple networks

Mastering a Cisco certification exam is not an easy task. Cisco has maintained the difficulty of the CCNA exam series by changing the exam requirements regularly. Some candidates pass the exam the first time; many pass it after multiple attempts, while some do not pass it. Good preparation is the best way to ensure that you pass the exam the first time.

Refer to
Figure
in online course

Before preparing for any certification examination, it is important to understand the purpose of the exam. Cisco certification examinations are designed to measure the knowledge, skills, and abilities of an individual in a defined area of expertise. The exams use a combination of techniques to enable a candidate to demonstrate readiness to perform various networking tasks. The exam can contain multiple choice questions, various exercises, and simulated network configuration tasks. Each question or task is designed to address a specific objective. The Cisco certification website lists the objectives for the ICND1 exam.

Cisco certification website

9.6.2 Networking Knowledge, Skills and Abilities

Refer to
Figure
in online course

To perform most networking tasks, some knowledge must be recalled from memory. This type of knowledge is made up of facts. When studying for a certification exam, identify the pertinent facts associated with each exam objective. Some individuals find it useful to create flashcards to help memorize these facts. While there may be a few questions on the exam that require the basic factual answers, more often the factual knowledge is needed to diagnose or solve a networking problem.

Refer to
Figure
in online course

Many skills are required when performing networking tasks. Some skills are fairly easy, such as creating and terminating a crossover cable. Other skills are more difficult, such as mastering IP subnetting.

The mastery of networking skills requires practice. Lab and Packet Tracer activities are designed to provide a structured practice environment for learners.

Cisco certifications measure and validate the networking skills of an individual based on how they interact with Cisco networking devices. Because of this, it is very important to practice with Cisco

Refer to
Figure
in online course

IOS software. Many exam tasks require the interpretation of Cisco IOS command output, especially the output of the various **show** commands.

The ability to plan, organize, execute, and problem solve is critical to the success of an entry-level network technician. In a certification exam environment, these abilities are usually measured using configuration and troubleshooting tasks. Effort is made when designing the exams to simulate conditions that an individual would find when performing an actual networking job. These conditions can be presented on the exam using scenarios or simulations.

Preparing for a scenario-based or simulation task is not as simple as memorizing a fact or practicing a specific skill. These types of tasks require an individual to apply both the facts and skills to solve a problem or meet a stated requirement.

One of the best ways to develop troubleshooting abilities is to start by analyzing what knowledge and skills are needed in order to perform specific networking tasks. When the necessary information is identified, anticipate what would happen if that information was not known. Make a list of the possible outcomes and determine what skills could be used to identify and correct any problems that may be created. That sounds difficult, but here are a few examples to consider:

- What would happen if a network technician did not know the correct number of host addresses available using a specific subnet mask? How could the problems be identified and corrected?

- What problems might arise in a RIPv2 network that has more than 15 hops from a source to a destination address? What would be a symptom of this problem? How could the problem be corrected?

Refer to
Interactive Graphic
in online course.

Activity

Match the item to the appropriate category.

Drag the task on the left to the appropriate category on the right.

Refer to
Lab Activity
for this chapter

Lab Activity

Identify the knowledge, skills, and abilities needed to perform the lab tasks.

9.6.3 Making the Commitment

Refer to
Figure
in online course

Getting ready to take a certification exam can be an overwhelming task. There is much information to review, many skills to practice, and pressure to succeed. Just like installing a network for a customer, exam preparation is more successful if it is broken down into a series of smaller steps:

1. Making the commitment.

2. Creating a plan.

3. Practicing test taking.

After you complete these steps, you are ready to begin the exam preparation.

Refer to
Figure
in online course

The first step to obtaining a Cisco certification is making the commitment to devote the time and effort necessary to prepare for the examination. This commitment needs to be assigned a top priority, because it will take time that was previously used for other activities.

In addition to taking time, preparing for a certification exam requires concentration. Find a place at home or at school where you can study for long periods of time uninterrupted. Trying to learn and practice networking skills can be extremely difficult if other distractions are present.

Having the right equipment and resources is also important. Make sure that you have access to a computer, the on-line course materials, and Packet Tracer software. Discuss with your instructor how to schedule lab time to practice your skills on actual equipment. Find out if remote lab access over the Internet is available in your area.

Inform friends and family of your commitment to obtaining the CCENT certification. Explain to them that their assistance and support are needed during the exam preparation. Even if they have no understanding of networking, they can help you study with flashcards or ask practice questions. At a minimum, they can help by respecting your need for uninterrupted study time. If others in your class are preparing for the exam at the same time, it may be helpful to organize a study group.

9.6.4 Creating a Plan

Refer to **Figure** in online course

After you have made the commitment to dedicate the time necessary to prepare to take the ICND1 examination, the next step is creating a plan. A certification preparation plan includes information on how you intend to prepare, a schedule of dates and times, and a list of the resources.

There are two ways to approach studying for a certification exam: individually or in a group. Many people find that creating a study group helps them to focus better on the material and keep to a schedule.

When studying with a partner or in a group, it is critical for all participants to know how to contact each other, the schedule and place for meetings, and other pertinent information. It may be necessary to assign members of the group different responsibilities, such as:

- Obtaining and distributing study materials

- Scheduling lab time

- Ensuring all necessary supplies are available

- Keeping track of the group progress

- Finding answers to problems

Studying alone might make the coordination of resources easier, but it does not diminish the importance of a good plan.

Refer to **Figure** in online course

Set a realistic target date for taking the exam based on the amount of time that is available each week to dedicate to the preparation.

Use smaller amounts of time for fact memorization, and larger blocks of time for practicing skills. It can be frustrating to begin a lab or skill practice exercise and not have sufficient time scheduled to complete it.

The Cisco Press CCENT study guide entitled "31 Days to the CCENT" can be used to structure a schedule. The book takes each exam objective and highlights the important information to study. It contains references to the sections and topics in the CCNA Discovery: Networking for Home and Small Businesses and CCNA Discovery: Working at a Small-to-Medium Business or ISP curriculum that need to be reviewed and practiced.

A good way to create a schedule is to record all of the available time on a calendar. Then assign each block of time to a specific task, such as "learn OSI model layers and their functions" or "practice IP subnetting." When all tasks are entered, determine when to schedule the exam.

Refer to **Figure** in online course

Investigate all the tools and resources that are available to help you study. The ICND1 tests the knowledge and skills obtained during this course, in addition to all the content from CCNA Discovery: Networking for Home and Small Businesses. Access to the online curriculum, labs, and Packet Tracer activities is critical to successful preparation.

In addition to these tools, many other study aids exist on the Cisco Learning Network. The link for the Cisco Learning Network is:

Cisco Learning Network

Cisco Press publishes a number of books that cover the CCENT exam objectives. These books can be purchased through the Cisco Marketplace Bookstore.

Cisco Marketplace Bookstore

After the necessary materials have been gathered, it is important to organize them. Reviewing and practicing the CCENT knowledge and skills can be difficult if it is approached in a haphazard manner. It is easier to recall and use information if it is learned and practiced in an organized framework.

9.6.5 Practicing Test Taking

Refer to
Figure
in online course

Recalling and performing networking skills in a formal testing environment is different from doing the same functions in a classroom or at home. It is important to understand the format of the exam and how it is administered.

Visit the Testing Center

Before taking the exam, visit the testing center and see how the exam is administered. Ask questions about what to expect. Some testing centers provide each examinee with a separate testing room; others have larger areas where a number of people are taking exams at the same time. Find out what is permitted to bring into the room and, more importantly, what items are not permitted. Visit the Cisco certification website to find the nearest testing center.

Format of the Examination

Certification exams are given online, similar to the manner in which Networking Academy assessments are delivered. There are, however, some differences:

- Survey questions may be presented before the actual examination begins. It is important to answer these questions truthfully. The survey questions have no impact on the content of the examination or on your final score.

- Certification exams are timed. The time remaining is displayed on the screen so that you can decide how long to spend on each question or task.

- There may be many different types of questions or tasks on the same examination.

- You cannot go back to a previous question after moving to the next one.

There is no way to skip a question or mark a question for review. If you do not know an answer, it is best to guess the answer and move on to the next question.

Refer to
Figure
in online course

Cisco certification exams include the following test formats:

- Multiple-choice single answer

- Multiple-choice multiple answer

- Drag-and-drop

- Fill-in-the-blank

- Testlet

- Simlet

■ Simulations

Before taking the exam, become familiar with how all question types function, especially the testlet, simlet, and simulation tool. This practice enables you to focus on the exam questions rather than on how to correctly use the tools. Practice the exam tutorial found on the Cisco Learning Network website until you are comfortable with the format and operation of each type of question and task.

Refer to
Lab Activity
for this chapter

Lab Activity

Use the Cisco Learning Network website to find study materials and tools to help prepare for the CCENT exam.

Refer to
Figure
in online course

Although nothing substitutes for the experience of taking the actual exam, it is often helpful to take practice exams. The Cisco Learning Network provides sample tests for the ICND1 exam that include multiple choice questions. If studying for the exam with other students, create practice questions and share them. In addition, there are commercially available practice exams that can be purchased and downloaded from the Internet.

Cisco certifications include tasks that simulate the operation of Cisco routers and switches. It is recommended that you repeat all Packet Tracers and Labs in this course in preparation for the ICND1 exam. However, just reading the curriculum and practicing the labs may not be adequate preparation for the types of integrated tasks that appear on a certification exam. It is important to investigate what might happen if there is an error in the setup or configuration of a device. Much can be learned by creating error situations and observing the changes in command output and device operation. Many of the scenario questions and tasks on the ICND1 exam are based on troubleshooting network problems.

Refer to **Packet
Tracer Activity**
for this chapter

Packet Tracer Activity

Use Telnet and other tools to troubleshoot problems in a small network.

9.6.6 Certification Study Guide

Refer to
Lab Activity
for this chapter

CCENT Study Guide

Click the lab icon to download a CCENT Preparation Guide for section 9.6.

Click the lab icon to download a CCENT Preparation Guide.

Refer to
Lab Activity
for this chapter

CCENT Study Guide

In addition to the previous Study Guide topics, the CCENT Certification also covers Wireless LANs (WLANs). This topic is covered in CCNA Discovery: Networking for Home and Small Businesses. For your convenience a Study Guide for WLANs is included here.

Click the lab icon to download a CCENT Study Guide for WLANs.

Chapter Summary

Click through the buttons for summary information.

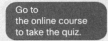

Chapter Quiz

Take the chapter quiz to check your knowledge.

Your Chapter Notes

10.0 Putting It All Together

Summary

Refer to
Figure
in online course

Packet Tracer Activity

Use the knowledge and skills presented in this course to perform a simulated network upgrade.

- Create an IP addressing plan for a small network
- Implement a network equipment upgrade
- Verify device configurations and network connectivity

View printable instructions.

Refer to
Figure
in online course

Lab Activity

Use the knowledge and skills presented in this course to perform this lab activity.

- Given a customer work order, implement a network upgrade.
- Review an existing customer network.
- Create an IP addressing scheme for the upgraded network.
- Create a physical diagram of the new network.
- Use a configuration checklist and configure networking devices.
- Use an installation checklist and connect the networking devices.
- Use a verification checklist and verify connectivity and routing table updates.

Refer to
Figure
in online course

This CCNA Discovery course is the second course in the Cisco Networking Academy Discovery course series. This course, along with the Networking for Home and Small Businesses course, has provided you with an opportunity to gain the knowledge, skills and abilities to prepare you to take the first exam in the Cisco Certified Network Associate Series.

In order to successfully pass the certification exam, you need to review the material presented in both courses. The Cisco certification exams require a hands-on component that is presented throughout the exam as simulations, which are similar to the e-labs contained within this course. Practice of all the hands-on labs and Packet Tracer activities is also recommended as preparation for the exam. Cisco provides an on-line certification preparation center, as well, to help ensure your success on the exam.

The Cisco Learning Network can be found at:

http://www.cisco.com/go/learningnetwork

To further your networking education, and to prepare for the Cisco CCNA exam, it is recommended that you continue through the last two courses in the CCNA Discovery Series:

Introducing Routing and Switching in the Enterprise - Learn how enterprise networks support critical business applications. Further refine and enhance your networking skills as you prepare for the Cisco CCNA certification.

Designing and Supporting Computer Networks - Learn the concepts that contribute to good network design. These skills prepare you for entry-level pre-sale positions with network vendors, as well as provide the fundamental knowledge necessary for students to start their own small network support businesses.

Your Chapter Notes

AAA

Authentication, Authorization, and Accounting Protocol specified in RFC 2903 and several other RFCs that determines who can access a system or network, how it can be accessed, and what activity occurs during the connection.

access control list

See ACL.

accounting

Tracking information about applications that are accessed, including by whom and the length of time that they are used.

ACK

acknowledgment

(1) Transmission control character or transmission frame that confirms that the data that was received was uncorrupted or without errors, or that the receiving station is ready to accept transmissions. (2) In TCP, ACK is used in the initial three-way handshake to acknowledge the sequence number of the sending station. Acknowledgment is also known as acknowledgement.

ACK packet

Type of message used in the TCP initial three-way handshake to acknowledge the sequence number of the sending station. When data is sent, the ACK packet confirms the data was received.

acknowledgment

See ACK.

ACL

access control list

(1) List managed by a network administrator that itemizes what a user is permitted to access and the type of access granted. (2) List kept by a network device, such as a router, to manage access to or from the router for a number of services. For example, an ACL can be used to prevent packets with a certain IP address or protocol from leaving a particular interface on the router.

AD

advertised distance

Distance that is broadcast by an upstream neighbor.

administrative distance

Rating of trustworthiness of a routing information source. For a Cisco router, administrative distance is expressed as a numerical value between 0 and 255. The higher the value, the lower the trustworthiness rating.

administrative domain

Group of hosts that belong to the same domain.

Address Resolution Protocol

See ARP.

administrative distance

See AD.

Advanced Encryption Standard

See AES.

AES

Advanced Encryption Standard

Symmetric 128-bit block cipher that replaces DES as the cryptographic standard for the U.S. government. AES is used with key sizes of 128 bits, 192 bits, or 256 bits, depending on the application security requirement.

alphanumeric character

Set of characters that includes letters and numbers.

analysis report

Information gathered by a design team of an service provider to determine the network requirements for a customer, such as the types of devices and cabling that are necessary.

antispam

Technique to prevent email spam delivery that can be implemented on a client or a server.

Application layer

Layer 7 of the OSI reference model that provides services to application processes such as email, file transfer, and terminal emulation that are outside of the OSI model. The Application layer identifies and establishes the resources required to connect with available communication partners. It establishes an agreement on procedures for error recovery and for control of data integrity. The Application layer interfaces directly to, and performs common application services for, the application processes.

archive-needed attribute

Feature in a computer file system that performs functions such as tracking changes to files for the purpose of backup or archiving.

ARP

Address Resolution Protocol
Standard used to identify the MAC address of a host when the IP address is known, by broadcasting an ARP request on the network. The host that has the IP address in the request then replies with its MAC address.

AS

Autonomous System
Group of networks under a common administration sharing a common routing strategy. Autonomous systems are subdivided by areas. An autonomous system must be assigned a unique 16-bit number by IANA.

ASN

Autonomous System Number
Identification of an AS for use when routing packets through the Internet.

authentication

Security measure designed to control access to network resources by verifying the identity of a person or process.

Authentication, Authorization, and Accounting

See AAA.

authorization

Permission to access specific resources and perform specific tasks.

autonomous system

See AS.

autonomous system number

See ASN.

back door

Method of bypassing normal authentication while attempting to remain hidden. A back door may be created by installing a program or by modifying a legitimate program.

bandwidth

(1) Amount of data that can be transmitted in a given period of time. (2) Difference between the highest and lowest frequencies available for network signals. (3) Rated throughput capacity of a given network medium or protocol.

BGP

Border Gateway Protocol
Exterior routing standard that supports route aggregation and is used to connect a service provider to the Internet.
Border Gateway Protocol replaced Exterior Gateway Protocol.

Border Gateway Protocol

See BGP.

broadcast

(1) Data packet that is sent to all nodes on a network. Compare broadcast with unicast and multicast. (2) Method for sending data packets to all devices on a network. Broadcasts are identified by a broadcast address and rely on routers to keep broadcasts from being sent to other networks.

buffer overflow attack

Condition triggered by malicious code where the data received is beyond the boundaries of a fixed-length buffer. The extra data overwrites adjacent memory locations.

byte

Unit of measure that identifies the size of a data file, the amount of space on a disk or other storage medium, or the amount of data being sent over a network. One byte consists of eight bits of data.

cable modem

Device that connects a computer to a cable company network through the same coaxial cabling that feeds CATV signals to a television set.

cable modem termination system
See CMTS.

CIDR

Classless Inter-Domain Routing
Technique supported by the BGP4 protocol and based on route aggregation. CIDR enables a router to group routes together to reduce the quantity of routing information carried by the core routers. With CIDR, a group of IP networks appear to be a single entity to networks outside of the group.

CiscoWorks

Internetwork management software, based on SNMP, used for monitoring router and access server status, managing configuration files, and troubleshooting network problems. CiscoWorks applications can be integrated on network management platforms such as SunNet Manager, HP OpenView, and IBM NetView.

classed address system

Method of classifying networks by the amount of bits used for the network portion of the address. There are five classes of networks: A, B, C, D, and E.

classful subnet

Extension of a subnet mask.

classless interdomain routing
See CIDR.

CMTS

Cable Modem Termination System
Device located at the local cable company that exchanges digital signals with cable modems on the Internet.

computer virus

Malicious software or code that can be replicated and may infect a computer without the knowledge or permission of the user. Some viruses do not adversely affect a computer, while other viruses can damage or delete operating system and data files.
A computer virus is also known as a virus.

connectionless

Data communication method or protocol that does not require an exchange of messages and does not require a pre-established correlation between source and destination. Compare connectionless with connection-oriented.

connection-oriented

Data communication method or protocol that requires the establishment of a virtual circuit. Compare connection-oriented with connectionless.

connectivity

Forming a network for access to resources and people by linking of devices and computers.

CPE

customer premises equipment
Terminating equipment, such as terminals, telephones, and modems that are supplied by the telephone company. A CPE is installed at a customer site and connected to the telephone company network.

custom subnet mask

32-bit address mask used to identify the bits of an IP address that are being used for the subnet address. Any subnet mask that is not a default class A, B or C subnet mask is considered a custom subnet mask.

customer premises equipment
See CPE.

DAS

direct-attached storage
Digital storage system that is attached to a host, such as a server or workstation. The connection between the DAS and the host may be SCSI or fiber-optic cable.
dual-attachment station
Device attached to both the primary and the secondary FDDI rings. Dual attachment provides redundancy for the FDDI ring. If the primary ring fails, the station switches to the secondary ring, which isolates the failure and retains ring integrity. Compare DAS with SAS. A dual-attachment station is also known as a Class A station.

data transfer process
See DTP.

datagram
Packets that are sent over a transmission medium without prior establishment of a virtual circuit, normally using UDP.

DDoS
distributed denial of service
Attack by multiple systems on a network that floods the bandwidth or resources of the targeted system, such as a web server, with the purpose to shut it down.

demilitarized zone
See DMZ.

denial of service
See DoS.

device log
Record of operations, processes, and configuration changes on a device. A device log should be maintained and reviewed as part of network maintenance.

DHCP
Dynamic Host Configuration Protocol
Standard used by a software utility that requests and assigns an IP address, default gateway, and DNS server address to a network host. DHCP allocates an IP address for a host dynamically so the address can be reused when the host no longer needs it.

dialup
Communications circuit that is established by a switched-circuit connection using a telephone company network.

differential backup
Copy of data saved onto storage media that has been created or modified since the last full backup. A differential backup does not reset the archive bit.

diffusing update algorithm
See DUAL.

digital encryption
Process that transforms data during transmission to prevent anyone but the intended recipient from being able to read the content.

digital subscriber line
See DSL.

direct-attached storage
See DAS.

distance vector
Class of routing algorithm that each router uses to broadcast or multicast route information to other nodes on the network. A router configured with a distance vector routing protocol evaluates the distance and direction to the destination to determine best path selection.

distributed denial of service
See DDoS.

distributed reflected denial of service
See DRDoS.

DMZ
demilitarized zone
Area in a network design that is located between the internal network and external network, usually the Internet. The DMZ is accessible to devices on the Internet, such as a web server, FTP server, SMTP server, and DNS.

DNS
Domain Name System
System that maps a host name, or URL, to an IP address.

Domain Name System
See DNS.

DoS
denial of service
Type of attack on a network when an abundance of requests for a resource is sent to cause the system to overload and cease to operate. DoS often target a system such as a web server with the purpose of shutting it down.
disk operating system
Programs and commands that control overall computer operations in a disk-based system. All letters are capitalized in the acronym for disk operating system: DOS

dot address

Common notation for an IP address in the form <a.b.c.d> where each number a represents, in decimal, 1 byte of the 4-byte IP address. Dot address is also known as dotted notation, dotted-decimal notation, and four-part dotted notation.

dotted-decimal notation

See dot address.

DRDoS

distributed reflected denial of service
Attack that involves sending a mock request to numerous computer systems on the Internet, with the source address of the request falsely modified as the targeted computer system. The targeted system becomes flooded as the numerous systems reply to the mock request.

DSL

digital subscriber line
Public network service that delivers high bandwidth at limited distances over the copper wiring of conventional telephone lines. DSL incorporates technology that enables devices to immediately connect to the Internet when powered on.

DTP

data transfer process
Method that establishes and manages the data connection.

DUAL

Diffusing Update Algorithm
Mathematical process used in EIGRP that provides loop-free operation at every instant throughout a route computation. DUAL allows routers involved in a topology change to synchronize at the same time, while not involving routers that are unaffected by the change.

Dynamic Host Configuration Protocol

See DHCP.

dynamic mapping

Process that occurs when a router is configured to assign an IP address from an available pool of outside global addresses to an inside private network device.

dynamic update

DNS process that automatically updates records in a Windows Server environment.

EAP

Extensible Authentication Protocol
Framework that supports multiple authentication mechanisms. In the negotiation process, EAP specifies the sequence of requests and responses between a client and an EAP enabled server until authentication is achieved. EAP is commonly used in WLANs.

e-commerce

electronic commerce
Buying and selling goods and services on the Internet.

EGP

Exterior Gateway Protocol
Standard for exchanging routing information between autonomous systems. EGP is an obsolete protocol that was replaced by BGP.

EIGRP

Enhanced Interior Gateway Routing Protocol
Proprietary Cisco routing protocol that combines distance vector routing protocol standards and link-state routing protocol standards. EIGRP uses DUAL to determine routing. EIGRP is also known as Enhanced IGRP.

encapsulation

Transmission of one network protocol within another. In tunneling, a data packet is encapsulated to form a new packet that conforms to the protocols used over intermediary networks. Tunneling is the basis of IP security systems such as IPSec used in VPNs.

encoding

Process of putting a sequence of characters, such as letters, numbers, punctuation, and certain symbols, into a specialized format for efficient transmission or storage.

Enhanced IGRP

See EIGRP.

enterprise

Any corporation, business, or other entity that uses computers in a networked environment. Enterprise usually refers to a large company or organization with complex networks. An enterprise network differs from a WAN because it is privately owned and maintained.

Extensible Authentication Protocol

See EAP.

Exterior Gateway Protocol

See EGP.

failure domain

Area of a network that is affected when a component of the network malfunctions or fails.

fault tolerance

Ability of a computer, server, or network to continue operating properly in the event of a failure of one or more of its components.

File Transfer Protocol

See FTP.

forward lookup

Type of DNS lookup that uses an Internet domain name to find an IP address. When a website address is entered into the browser address field, it is translated to an IP address used by routers to contact the web server.

FQDN

fully qualified domain name

Complete expression of the location of a host or server on the Internet. An FQDN includes both the host name and the domain name.

FTP

File Transfer Protocol

Application standard used for transferring files between network nodes. FTP is defined in RFC 959 and is part of the TCP/IP protocol stack.

FTPS

Secure File Transfer Protocol

FTP with SSL security. FTPS uses encryption, control, and management features to provide secure and reliable data transfers.

full backup

Copy of all files on a disk saved onto storage media for the purpose of restoring the data and computer operations in case of data loss. Full backup is also known as normal backup.

fully qualified domain name

See FQDN.

hierarchy

System of organizing components in multilevel or tiered arrangement to facilitate grouping.

high-order bit

First few bits, either 1s or 0s, of the first octet of an IP address when written in binary. The high order bits are used to indicate the class of an IP address. If the first bit of the first octet is set to a 0, the IP address is Class A. To determine if an address is Class A, a device must only examine the first bit; therefore, class A addresses have a high-order bit of 0. If the first bit of the first octet is set to 1, the device must examine the second bit to determine the class. If the second bit is set to 0, the IP address is Class B. In this case, the high-order bits are 10. If the first bit is set to 1, and the second is set to 1, the device must examine the third bit. If the third is set to 0, the IP address is Class C and the high-order bits are 110. If the first bit is set to 1, the second is set to 1, the third is set to 1, and the fourth is set to 0, the IP address is Class D, and the high-order bits are 1110. If the first bit is set to 1, the second bit is set to 1, the third bit is set to 1, and the fourth bit is set to 1, the IP address is Class E, and the high-order bits are 1111.

hop

Transfer of a data packet between two network devices, such as routers.

hop count

Routing metric that tracks the number of legs that a data packet traverses between a source and a destination. RIP uses hop count as its sole metric.

host ID

host identification

Portion of a logical address that identifies an individual host on a network.

HTTP

Hypertext Transfer Protocol

Standard used to transfer or convey information on the World Wide Web. HTTP is a communication protocol that establishes a request/response connection on the Internet.

HTTP 1.1

Hypertext Transfer Protocol 1.1

Recent version of HTTP that provides faster delivery of web pages than the original HTTP and reduces web traffic.

HTTPS

Secure Hypertext Transfer Protocol

Standard that provides secure internet file transfers using SSL to add encryption and other security features to HTTP activities.

hyperlink

Element in an HTML document that links to another location in the same document or to an entirely different document.

Hypertext Transfer Protocol

See HTTP.

Hypertext Transfer Protocol 1.1

See HTTP 1.1.

ICMP

Internet Control Message Protocol

Standard for network layer testing and troubleshooting. ICMP provides the ability to report diagnostic and error messages. The ping command is part of the ICMP utility.

IDS

intrusion detection system

Device with a sensor, console, and central engine that is installed on a network to protect against attacks missed by a conventional firewall. IDS inspects all inbound and outbound network activity and identifies suspicious patterns that may indicate a network or system attack. It is configured to send an alarm to network administrators when such attack is encountered.

IETF

Internet Engineering Task Force

Task force consisting of over 80 working groups responsible for developing Internet standards. The IETF is part of Internet Society, or ISOC.

IGP

Interior Gateway Protocol

Standard used to exchange routing information within an autonomous system. Examples of an Internet IGP includes EIGRP, OSPF, and RIP.

IMAP

Internet Message Access Protocol

Application Layer standard that enables a local client to access email on a remote server.

IMAP4

Internet Message Access Protocol 4

Application Layer standard that enables a local client to access email on a remote server. Messages are downloaded to the client but kept on the server. IMAP4 is an updated version of IMAP.

incident management

Procedure that should be followed when a help desk technician initiates a problem solving process.

incremental backup

Copy of data saved onto storage media for the purpose of restoring the data and computer operations in case of data loss. An incremental backup occurs only on files and folders that have been created or modified since the last full backup.

inside global address

Public-routable IP address of an inside host as it appears to the outside network. Inside global address is an IP address translated by NAT.

inside local address

Private IP address configured on a host on an inside network. An inside local address must be translated before it can travel outside the local addressing structure to the Internet.

inside local network

Privately addressed network space connected to a router interface. Inside local network is used to overcome shortages of public IP addressing.

Integrated Services Digital Network

See ISDN.

Interior Gateway Protocol

See IGP.

Internet

Internetwork that connects networks worldwide. The Internet evolved in part from ARPANET.
Internet is an abbreviation for internetwork.

Internet Control Message Protocol

See ICMP.

Internet Engineering Task Force

See IETF.

Internet Message Access Protocol

See IMAP.

Internet Message Access Protocol 4

See IMAP4.

Internet Protocol

See IP.

Internet Protocol address

See IP address.

Internet service provider

See ISP.

intrusion detection system

See IDS.

intrusion prevention system

See IPS.

IP

Internet Protocol
Network Layer standard in the TCP/IP stack for connectionless internetwork service. IP provides features for addressing, type-of-service specification, fragmentation and reassembly, and security. IP is defined in RFC 791.

IP address

Internet Protocol address
(1) 32-bit address in IPv4 that is assigned to hosts that use TCP/IP. An IP address belongs to one of five classes: A, B, C, D, or E. An IP address is written with four octets in the dot address format <a.b.c.d>. Each address consists of a network number, an optional subnetwork number, and a host number. The network and subnetwork numbers together are used for routing. The host number is used to address an individual host within the network or subnetwork. A subnet mask is used to extract network and subnetwork information from the IP address.
(2) Command used to establish the logical network address of this interface.

IP address pool

Internet Protocol address pool
Range of registered IP addresses to be used with NAT.

IP Security

See IPSec.

IPS

intrusion prevention system
Software that prevents an attack to data on a network. An IPS is an extension of the IDS.

IPSec

Internet Protocol Security
Framework for open standards that provides data confidentiality, data integrity, and data authentication between participating peers. IPSec protects one or more data flows between a pair of hosts, between a pair of security gateways, or between a security gateway and a host. It uses IKE to handle the negotiation of protocols and algorithms. IPSec provides security services at the IP layer.

IPv6

Internet Protocol version 6
Network Layer standard for packet-switched internetworks to which all TCP/IP hosts might eventually migrate. IPv6 uses a 128-bit addressing structure. IPv6 is the successor of IPv4 for general use on the Internet.

ISDN

Integrated Services Digital Network

Communications protocol that permits telephone networks to carry data, voice, and other source traffic.

ISP

Internet service provider

Organization, such as the local phone or cable company, that provides Internet service to home users.

LAN

local-area network

High-speed, low-error data transfer system that encompasses a small geographic area. A LAN connects workstations, peripherals, terminals, and other devices in a single building or other geographically limited area. LAN standards specify cabling and signaling at the Physical Layer and the Data Link Layer of the OSI reference model. Examples of LAN technologies are Ethernet, FDDI, and Token Ring.

LAND attack

Local-Area Network Denial of Service attack

Type of security attack that can cause a computer to become locked. The corrupt packet that is sent to a device uses the same IP address for both the source and the destination which causes the computer to continuously reply to itself.

LAND attack is also known as Local-Area Network DoS attack, or LanD attack.

link state

Class of routing algorithm that updates neighbors based on changes in the network topology using link state information. Link-state information includes the interface IP address/subnet mask, the status of a link, the type of network, the cost of the link, and neighboring routers on that link. A router that is configured with a link-state routing protocol evaluates the cost of the links toward the destination to determine best path selection.

link-local address

IP address in the range from 169.254.1.0 to 169.254.254.255.

link-state advertisement

See LSA.

local traffic

Packets generated and managed by routers and routing protocols. Local traffic stays within an autonomous system.

local-area network

See LAN.

Local-Area Network DoS attack

See LAND attack.

logical topology

Map of the devices and the flow of data on a network. A logical topology demonstrates how the devices communicate with each other. Compare logical topology with physical topology.

LSA

link-state advertisement

Broadcast packet used by link-state protocols that contains information about neighbors and path costs. LSAs are used by the receiving routers to maintain their routing tables.

A link-state advertisement is also known as a link-state packet.

main distribution facility

See MDF.

malware

Software designed to infiltrate or damage a computer system.

MAN

metropolitan-area network

Network that spans a metropolitan area. Generally, a MAN spans a larger geographic area than a LAN, but a smaller geographic area than a WAN.

managed service

Service provider that offers onsite support of a customer network.

management information base

See MIB.

management VLAN

management virtual-area network

VLAN that is configured on a switch used for management purposes. The switch IP address is assigned to the management VLAN and is used to access and configure the switch remotely and to exchange information with other network devices. By default, the management VLAN on a switch is VLAN1.

MBSA

Microsoft Baseline Security Analyzer

Microsoft tool that helps analyze security problems in Microsoft Windows by scanning for security problems found in the operating system and Windows components such as IIS web server, Microsoft SQL Server, and Microsoft Office.

MDF

Main Distribution Facility

Primary communications room for a building. An MDF is the central point of a star networking topology where patch panels, hubs, and routers are located. It is used to connect public or private lines coming into the building to internal networks.

mean time between failures

See MTBF.

mean time to repair

See MTTR.

medium

Physical material on which data is transferred. UTP cable is a form of networking media.

message payload

Contents of a message.

metric

Information that a routing algorithm uses to determine the best route on a network. Metrics are stored in a routing table. Metrics include bandwidth, communication cost, delay, hop count, load, MTU, path cost, and reliability.

Metro Ethernet

Network system based on Ethernet technology that covers a metropolitan area. Metro Ethernet is commonly used as a MAN to connect subscribers and businesses to a WAN, such as the Internet.

metropolitan-area network

See MAN.

MIB

Management Information Base

Database used and maintained by network management protocols, such as SNMP and CMIP. The value of a MIB object can be changed or retrieved using SNMP or CMIP commands. MIB objects are organized into a tree structure that has public, standard branches and private, proprietary branches.

Microsoft Baseline Security Analyzer

See MBSA.

MTBF

mean time between failures

Average length of time that the device will work without failing. The MTBF is used to estimate the average life span of a hard disk and other computer elements.

MTTR

mean time to repair

Calculation of the length of time a device will take to recover from a non-terminal failure. In a maintenance contract, a system with a shorter MTTR is more expensive.

multicast

Single packet copied by the network and sent to a specific subset of network addresses which are specified in the destination address field. Compare multicast with broadcast and unicast.

NAP

Network Access Point

Obsolete locations for the interconnection of Internet service providers in the United States.

NAS

network-attached storage
High-speed, high-capacity data storage that groups large numbers of disk drives that are directly attached to the network and can be used by any server. A NAS device is typically attached to an Ethernet network and is assigned its own IP address.

NAT

Network Address Translation
Standard used to reduce the number of IP addresses necessary for all nodes within the organization to connect to the Internet. NAT allows a large group of private users to access the Internet by converting packet headers for only a small pool of public IP addresses and keeping track of them in a table.

network access point
See NAP.

Network Address Translation
See NAT.

network ID

network identification
Portion of a logical address that identifies the network to which the host belongs.

network-attached storage
See NAS.

normal backup
See full backup.

object identifier
See OID.

octet

Eight consecutive bits that are considered as a unit. Instead of a 8-digit binary number, the corresponding decimal or hexadecimal numbers can be used. For instance, the octet "11011100" can be written as the decimal number "220". Octets range in mathematical value from 0 to 255.

octet boundary

Boundary between four 8-bit octets in a 32-bit IPv4 address. Network classes A, B and C change on the boundaries.

OID

Number used to define an object in a MIB.

Open Shortest Path First
See OSPF.

optical media

Video disc that stores data in digital format. The content on optical media is written and read using laser technology. Examples of optical media include CD and DVD.

OSPF

Open Shortest Path First
Routing algorithm for a link-state, hierarchical IGP that replaces RIP. OSPF features include least-cost routing, multipath routing, and load balancing.

outside global address

Public IP address of an external host allocated from a globally routable address or network space.

outside global network

Any network attached to the router that is external to the LAN and that does not recognize private addresses assigned to hosts on the LAN.

outside local address

IP address of an outside host as it appears to hosts on the inside network.

packet

Logical grouping of information which includes a header that contains control information and user data. The term packet is used to refer to Network Layer units of data.

PAT

Port Address Translation
Standard used to reduce the number of internal private IP addresses to only one or a few external public IP addresses. PAT enables an organization to conserve addresses in the global address pool by allowing source ports in TCP connections or UDP conversations to be translated. Different local addresses then map to the same global address, with PAT providing the unique information. PAT is a subset of NAT functionality.

persistent connection

Method that enables one HTTP connection to send and receive multiple HTTP requests and responses. For example, when a website is accessed, the browser downloads the index.html file, as well as the images and files referenced in the HTML file. Persistent connection was introduced to HTTP 1.1.

phishing

Type of spam intended to persuade the recipient to provide the sender with access to personal information.

physical topology

Layout of devices on a network. The physical topology is the connection and arrangement of devices and cabling. Compare physical topology with logical topology.

PI

protocol interpreter

Control connection between an FTP client and an FTP server. The PI establishes a TCP connection and passes control information to the server.

point of presence

See POP.

POP

Point of Presence

Physical location at an ISP where local subscriber connections are authenticated and switched or routed to other locations.

Post Office Protocol

Standard used to enable access to email messages from a server.

POP3

Post Office Protocol version 3

Application Layer Internet standard that enables a local client to retrieve email from a remote server over a TCP/IP connection.

port

(1) Interface on an internetworking device, such as a router. (2) In IP terminology, an upper-layer process that is receiving information from lower layers. (3) To rewrite software or microcode so that it will run on a different hardware platform or in a different software environment

than that for which it was originally designed. (4.) Female plug on a patch panel which accepts the same size plug as an RJ45 jack. A patch cord is used in ports to cross connect computers that are wired to the patch panel. It is this cross connection that enables the LAN to function.

Port Address Translation

See PAT.

port filter

Practice of access control by selectively enabling or disabling TCP and UDP ports.

port number

Identification of a process on a computer using TCP or UDP.

Post Office Protocol

See POP.

Post Office Protocol version 3

See POP3.

pre-shared key

See PSK.

private network address

Portion of an IP address that is reserved for internal use. A private network address is not routed across the public Internet. In IPv4, the range of private network addresses are 10.0.0.0 to 10.255.255.255, 172.16.0.0 to172.31.255.255, and 192.168.0.0 to 192.168.255.255.

private peer

Direct connection between two or more ISPs that allows them to switch Internet traffic at no cost.

production environment

Software, equipment, documentation, and procedures used in support of business operations when a network is brought into service.

protocol interpreter

See PI.

prototype

Implementation of a portion of a network to prove the design meets the requirements for a larger network.

proxy service

Connection provided by a server that stands in for another server. A client connects to a proxy server to request resources that are available from another server.

PSK

pre-shared key
Secret code shared between a wireless access point and a client. The pre-shared key is used to control access to a network.

public peer

Process that enables multiple ISPs to interconnect across a single physical port, known as an exchange point.

queue

(1) Ordered list of elements waiting to be processed. (2) In routing, a backlog of packets waiting to be forwarded over a router interface.

reachability

Measurement used by a routing protocol to determine whether a remote network is accessible.

reachability information

Measurement of how accessible a network is. Reachability information is exchanged by exterior routing protocols, such as BGP.

reliable

Guarantee that a message will be delivered. Reliable refers to the ability of a system or component to perform its required functions under stated conditions for a specified period of time.

reverse lookup

Process to determine the hostname or host associated with a given IP address or host address.

RFC 1918

Request for Comments 1918
Standard for private network space and the use of private addressing on a network.

RIP

Routing Information Protocol
Distance vector routing standard that uses hop count as a routing matrix.

route cost

Value based on hop count, media bandwidth, or other measures that is assigned by a network administrator and used to compare paths through an internetwork environment.

routing algorithm

Mathematical formula and procedures used to determine the best route for traffic from a particular source to a particular destination.

Routing Information Protocol
See RIP.

SAN

storage-area network
Data communication platform that interconnects servers and storage at Gigabaud speeds. By combining LAN networking models with server performance and mass storage capacity, SAN eliminates bandwidth issues and scalability limitations created by previous SCSI bus-based architectures.

SAS

single-attachment station
Device attached only to the primary ring of an FDDI ring. Compare SAS with DAS. SAS is also known as a Class B station.

scalability

Feature of a network design to include new user groups and remote sites over time. A scalable network design should support new applications without impacting the level of service delivered to existing users.

second-level domain

Portion of IP address that is directly below a top-level domain. For example, in cisco.com, "cisco" is a second-level domain of the .com. A second-level domain refers to the organization that registered the domain name with a domain name registrar.

Secure File Transfer Protocol
See FTPS.

Secure Hypertext Transfer Protocol
See HTTPS.

Secure Socket Layer
See SSL.

segment

(1) Section of a network that is bounded by bridges, routers, or switches. (2) In a LAN using a bus topology, a segment is a continuous electrical circuit that is often connected to other such segments with repeaters. (3) Term used in the TCP specification to describe a single transport layer unit of information. The terms datagram, frame, message, and packet are also used to describe logical information groupings at various layers of the OSI reference model and in various technology circles.

serial cable

External cable that connects the serial port on the computer to a peripheral device.

server farm

Group of servers located in a central facility and maintained by the central group to provide server needs for organizations. A server farm usually has primary and backup server hardware for load balancing, redundancy, and fault tolerance purposes. Server farm architecture provides the operation and maintenance of servers.

Service Level Agreement

See SLA.

Shortest Path First

See SPF.

signature

Pattern that the security tool in anti-virus and intrusion detection systems looks for when scanning files or network traffic.

Simple Mail Transfer Protocol

See SMTP.

Simple Network Management Protocol

See SNMP.

single-attachment station

See SAS.

SLA

Service Level Agreement

Contract that defines expectations between an organization and the service vendor to provide an agreed upon level of support.

SMTP

Simple Mail Transfer Protocol

Email standard that enables a server to send ASCII text messages. To include pictures and documents in an email, SMTP is augmented by the MIME protocol. SMTP can be used to retrieve messages from an email server, however IMAP or POP are preferred.

SNMP

Simple Network Management Protocol

Standard that enables individual devices on a network to be monitored. SNMP-compliant devices use agents to monitor predefined parameters for specific conditions. These agents collect information and store it in a MIB. SNMP is used almost exclusively in TCP/IP networks.

socket

Communication end-point that uniquely identifies a particular application process running on an individual host device. A socket pair is made up of source and destination IP addresses and port numbers.

solid state storage

Type of nonvolatile memory device, such as a Flash drive, that uses integrated circuits rather than magnetic or optical media.

SP

synchronization packet

Initial packet sent in a TCP three-way handshake. The SYN packet is used to request a TCP session with another end-point.

service provider

Organization, such as the local phone or cable company, that provides Internet service.

switch processor

Cisco 7000-series processor module that acts as the administrator for all CxBus activities.

A switch processor is also known as a ciscoBus controller.

spam

Unsolicited or junk email messages sent to multiple recipients for either legitimate or fraudulent purposes.

SPF

Shortest Path First

Mathematical process used to determine the shortest path to a destination by identifying all paths and the total cost of each path. SPF is commonly used in link-state routing algorithms.

SPF is also known as Dijkstra's algorithm.

spyware

Malware that monitors the activity of a computer on a network, typically without a user's knowledge or permission. Spyware captures keystrokes and sends the information to the organization responsible for launching the spyware.

SSL

Secure Socket Layer

Protocol used to provide secure communications on the Internet such as web browsing, e-mail, Internet faxing, instant messaging, and other data transfers. SSL uses a cryptographic system with two keys to encrypt data: a public key known as a digital certificate, and a private, or secret key known only to the recipient of the message.

stack

Reference to a protocol stack which is a group of protocols that work together to facilitate network communication.

static map

Tool used to establish communication with a device outside of the network. A static map is used in the process to translate an unregistered, private IP address to a registered, pubic IP address.

static NAT

Static Network Address Translation

Type of translation protocol used by an internal host with a fixed private IP address to continually map to a fixed public IP address.

storage-area network

See SAN.

stream

Continuous transmission of data from one location to another. Streaming video is the continuous, real-time flow of the video being downloaded.

strengths weaknesses opportunities threats

See SWOT.

subnet

(1) System in an IP network that shares a particular subnet address. A subnetwork is arbitrarily segmented by a network administrator to provide a multilevel, hierarchical routing structure while shielding the subnetwork from the addressing complexity of attached networks.
(2) In an OSI network, a collection of end and intermediate systems under the control of a single administrative domain and using a single network access protocol.

Subnet is also known as subnetwork.

subnet mask

32-bit address mask used to identify the bits of an IP address that are being used for the subnet address. A subnet mask identifies the network portion, the subnet portion, and the host portion of an IP address.

SWOT

strengths, weaknesses, opportunities, or threats

Part of the planning process in network design that evaluates the strengths, weaknesses, opportunities, and threats to a network or network upgrade.

SYN flood

Type of denial-of-service attack that randomly opens TCP ports and overloads network equipment and computer resources with a large amount of false requests, causing sessions to be denied to others.

SYN packet

See SP.

synchronization packet

See SP.

syslog

Client/server protocol that is used for forwarding network and security event messages. A syslog server is configured to receive real time messages from syslog enabled clients.

syslog daemon

Syslog server that receives messages from syslog senders.

T3 connection

Circuit channel that carries multiple T1 channels that are multiplexed, resulting in transmission rates of up to 44.736 Mbps. T3 cabling is used for Internet backbone cabling and to connect service providers to the backbone.

TCP

Transmission Control Protocol
Primary standard for the delivery of data. TCP is used for end-to-end connection establishment, error detection and recovery, and metering the rate of data flow into the network. Many standard applications, such as email, web browser, file transfer, and Telnet, depend on the services of TCP.

TCP/IP

Transmission Control Protocol/Internet Protocol
Set of public standards that specifies how packets of information are exchanged between copmuters over one or more networks. TCP and IP are the two primary protocols on which the Internet is based.

telecommunications room

Facility that maintains network and telecommunications equipment, vertical and horizontal cable terminations, and cross-connect cables. A telecommunications room is also known as a riser, a distribution facility, or a wiring closet.

Temporal Key Integrity Protocol
See TKIP.

TFTP

Trivial File Transfer Protocol
Standards that enables files to be transferred from one computer to another over a network, usually without client authentication. TFTP is a simplified version of FTP.

three-way handshake

Process that establishes a TCP session between two endpoints. A three-way handshake is a series of synchronization and acknowledgments used by TCP to open a connection. A client sends a segment with a SYN flag. The server responds with à SYN-ACK. The client then sends back an ACK, known as a SYN-ACK-ACK, and the session is established.

throughput

Rate at which a computer or network sends or receives data measured in bits per second.

Tier 1

Type of service provider connected directly to the Internet backbone that is also considered part of the backbone.

Tier 2

Type of service provider that covers limited geographical areas and purchases Internet access from Tier 1 service providers.

Tier 3

Type of service provider that typcially covers a smaller geographical area than a Tier 2 and purchases Internet access from Tier 1 or Tier 2 service providers.

tiered backup

Disaster recovery strategy that identifies methods for preserving mission-critical data that is required for business continuity planning.

TKIP

Temporal Key Integrity Protocol
WPA standard used to ensure integrity in wireless data transmission.

TLD

top-level domain
In the DNS heirarachy, the highest level of grouping for an internet host. It is the last part of an Internet domain name. Examples of TLDs include .com, .mil, .gov. For example, in cisco.com, "com" is the TLD.

TLS

Transport Layer Security
Encryption protocol used for secure communications between client/server processes. TLS is a predecessor to SSL.

top-level domain
See TLD.

topological database
Information received from routers that is used to build a routing table and determine the best path to a destination network.

traffic
Packets that traverse through a router or network at one time.

transit traffic
Packets generated by outside hosts or routers that travel through one autonomous system destined for another autonomous system. A border gateway is used to allow or deny transit traffic.

Transmission Control Protocol
See TCP.

Transmission Control Protocol/Internet Protocol
See TCP/IP.

Transport Layer Security
See TLS.

trap
Message sent by an SNMP agent to a network management system, console, or terminal indicating that a significant event, such as a specially defined condition or a threshold has been reached.

triggered update
Updated information sent out by a router when a change in the network occurs.

Trivial File Transfer Protocol
See TFTP.

Trojan Horse
Malicious code concealed in an application that is installed by a hacker with access to a computer on a network. When the application is run, the Trojan Horse damages data on the computer.

UDP
User Datagram Protocol
Connectionless transport layer protocol in the TCP/IP protocol stack. UDP is a simple protocol that exchanges datagrams without acknowl-

edgments or guaranteed delivery. It is a connectionless service for delivery of data with less overhead than TCP and designed for speed. Network management applications, network file systems, and simple file transport use UDP. Compare UDP with TCP.

unicast
Type of message sent to a single network destination. Compare unicast with broadcast and multicast.

User Datagram Protocol
See UDP.

virtual local-area network
See VLAN.

virtual private network
See VPN.

VLAN
virtual local-area network
Logical group of devices on a network that may or may not be in the same physical location.

VPN
Virtual Private Network
Encryption system that protects data as it travels, or tunnels, over the Internet or other unsecured public network.

WAN
wide-area network
Data communication network that serves users across a broad geographic area and often uses transmission devices provided by common carriers. Examples of WAN technologies include Frame Relay, SMDS, and X.25.

WEP
Wired Equivalent Privacy
Optional security mechanism defined within the 802.11 standard designed to make the link integrity of wireless devices equal to that of a cable. WEP is a first-generation security standard for wireless technology and provides a low level of security.

wide-area network
See WAN.

Wi-Fi Protected Access
See WPA.

Wired Equivalent Privacy
See WEP.

wireless LAN
See WLAN.

Wireshark
Packet sniffing application used for network troubleshooting and analysis. Wireshark captures packets coming into or going out of the NIC and decodes the packet contents for readability.

WLAN
wireless local-area network
Two or more computers or devices equipped to use spread-spectrum technology based on radio waves for communication within a limited area. WLAN is also know as wireless LAN.

worm
Computer program that can run independently and can propagate a complete working version of itself onto other hosts on a network. A worm can consume computer resources, such as network bandwidth, memory, and storage space.

WPA
Wi-Fi Protected Access
Security model based on the IEEE 802.11i standard. WPA is an interoperable security enhancement that provides security in a wireless network. Provides better encryption and authentication than earlier WEP system.

zone
(1) Logical group of network devices in AppleTalk. (2) Portion of the global DNS namespace.

CCNA Discovery
learning resources

Cisco Press, the authorized publisher for the Cisco® Networking Academy®, has a variety of learning and preparation tools to help you master the knowledge and prepare successfully for the CCENT™ and CCNA® exams.

From foundational learning to late-stage review, practice, and preparation, the varied print, software, and video products from Cisco Press can help you with learning, mastering, and succeeding!

Learning Guides

Learning Guides provide the textbook and labs all together as one resource per course.

Networking for Home and Small Business, CCNA Discovery Learning Guide	1587132095 / 9781587132094
Working at a Small-to-Medium Business or ISP, CCNA Discovery Learning Guide	1587132109 / 9781587132100
Introducing Routing and Switching in the Enterprise, CCNA Discovery Learning Guide	1587132117 / 9781587132117
Designing and Supporting Computer Networks, CCNA Discovery Learning Guide	1587132125 / 9781587132124

Other CCENT and CCNA resources

Books, software, and network simulations to help you prepare

31 Days before your CCENT Certification	1587132176 / 9781587132179
31 Days Before your CCNA Exam, Second Edition	1587131978 / 9781587131974
CCNA Official Exam Certification Library, Third Edition	1587201836 / 9781587201837
CCNA Portable Command Guide, Second Edition	1587201933 / 9781587201936
CCNA 640-802 Network Simulator (from Pearson Certification)	1587202166 / 9781587202162
CCNA 640-802 Cert Flash Cards Online	1587202212/9781587202216

For more information on this and other Cisco Press products, visit www.ciscopress.com/academy

Cisco Press

Learning is Serious Business. **Invest Wisely.**